THE ULTIMATE
COOKING
FOR ONE
COOKBOOK

No Waste, Great Taste!

175 Super Easy Recipes Made Just for You

Joanie Zisk of OneDishKitchen.com

Adams Media
New York London Toronto Sydney New Delhi

DEDICATION

To my husband EJ and my children. Without their loving support, this book would not have become a reality. Also, to my readers: I want you to enjoy cooking for yourself because you are worth it.

Adams Media
An Imprint of Simon & Schuster, Inc.
100 Technology Center Drive
Stoughton, MA 02072

First Adams Media trade paperback edition December 2019

ADAMS MEDIA and colophon are trademarks of Simon & Schuster.

For information about special discounts for bulk purchases, please contact Simon & Schuster Special Sales at 1-866-506-1949 or business@simonandschuster.com.

The Simon & Schuster Speakers Bureau can bring authors to your live event. For more information or to book an event contact the Simon & Schuster Speakers Bureau at 1-866-248-3049 or visit our website at www.simonspeakers.com.

Interior design by Julia Jacintho
Interior images © 123RF/Mariia Dolhova, chelovector
Photographs by James Stefiuk
Author photograph by Two Eleven Photography

Manufactured in the United States of America

9 2023

Library of Congress Cataloging-in-Publication Data
Names: Zisk, Joanie, author.
Title: The ultimate cooking for one cookbook / Joanie Zisk of OneDishKitchen.com.
Description: Avon, Massachusetts: Adams Media, 2019.
Includes index.
Identifiers: LCCN 2019035115 | ISBN 9781507211380 (pb) | ISBN 9781507211397 (ebook)
Subjects: LCSH: Cooking for one. | LCGFT: Cookbooks.
Classification: LCC TX714 .Z57 2019 | DDC 641.5/611--dc23
LC record available at https://lccn.loc.gov/2019035115

ISBN 978-1-5072-1138-0
ISBN 978-1-5072-1139-7 (ebook)

CV 09.28.2023 1030

TABLE OF CONTENTS

INTRODUCTION

Life gets pretty busy. And between all of the appointments, work projects, and errands, the thought of cooking can feel overwhelming—especially when there is just one of you and it seems like every recipe is for four or more people. Food can often go to waste, and that is enough to have you reaching for a takeout menu. Fortunately, making a single-serving or small-batch recipe that you want to enjoy for a specific meal takes less time, and gives you the freedom to change things up every day and not accumulate a lot of leftovers that will just be thrown away later.

In *The Ultimate Cooking for One Cookbook*, I've curated 175 of my favorite easy, flavorful, and waste-free recipes that you're sure to love. Organized into chapters by course, you'll discover new go-to recipes for every meal—from grab-and-go breakfasts like Fruit-Filled Overnight Oats (see recipe in Chapter 2), to delicious meat and seafood entrées like Lemon and Garlic Chicken (see recipe in Chapter 4) and Baked Stuffed Fish Fillet (see recipe in Chapter 6), to satisfying vegetarian options such as Spicy Stir-Fried Zucchini (see recipe in Chapter 7). And if you've got a craving for dessert, you'll absolutely love the single-serving Lemon Meringue Pie (see recipe in Chapter 8)!

But before you pull out your cutting board and fire up the oven, take a look at the first chapter on the basics of cooking for one. Here, you'll learn more about both prepping for and creating single-serving and small-batch meals, from which cooking accessories will come in handy, to what ingredients you'll want to stock your kitchen with.

When you have accessible ingredients and easy, delicious recipes on hand, you can create and enjoy a fabulous meal for one in no time. Whether you live alone, you're a parent who wants to indulge while the kids enjoy their own favorites, or you have a partner who travels, *The Ultimate Cooking for One Cookbook* is for you! Enjoy!

CHAPTER ONE
SIMPLE WAYS TO COOK FOR ONE

Not everyone starts out loving to cook. For some, including famous chef Julia Child, who confessed that she didn't know how to cook until she was in her thirties, learning and loving cooking takes time—and a little shift in mind-set. The truth is that preparing a meal for yourself can often feel like a chore tacked onto a very long list of other to-dos you are tempted to put off. However, it doesn't have to be a hassle, nor do you have to spend weeks working through the same tired leftovers (or throwing them away altogether). In fact, it can be one of the most enjoyable and healthy things you do for yourself!

In this chapter, you will begin your journey into simple, joyful cooking for one. You'll first explore the essential tools and techniques for creating your best single-serving and small-batch dishes. Then, you'll learn more about how to avoid wasting food (the biggest home-cooking pitfall for many!) and what ingredients are a must-have in every kitchen. After taking a look through this handy list, you'll discover a quick guide to properly reading a recipe, so you can avoid classic slipups like measuring ingredients before sifting them when a recipe calls for sifting first. From important pans and the best seasonings, to determining recipe doneness, this chapter is your crash course in cooking for one.

Essential Kitchen Equipment

You don't need a lot of fancy gadgets or special utensils to cook for yourself, but there are some pans and baking dishes you should have in certain sizes in order to make delicious small-batch and single-serving recipes at home. Cook times can vary depending on the size of dishes, and the recipes in this book have been developed and tested using the dish sizes that follow. Discount stores and thrift stores are great places to find small baking dishes and gently used pans:

- 8" ovenproof skillet
- 10" ovenproof skillet
- 1-quart saucepan
- 2-quart saucepan
- 5" baking dish
- 8-ounce ramekin
- 6.5" cast-iron skillet
- 9.5" baking dish or loaf pan
- 6-cup muffin pan
- 13" × 10" rimmed baking sheet

Other Kitchen Equipment

In addition to the essentials, there are a few other tools you should have on-hand when cooking. From mixing bowls to a silicone spatula, the following equipment will make your kitchen experiences run as smoothly as possible:

- Immersion (or stick) blender
- Digital scale
- Kitchen knives, including a chef's knife, paring knife, and bread knife
- Hand mixer
- Measuring spoons and cups
- Mixing bowls
- Large, durable cutting board
- Silicone spatula
- Balloon whisk
- Spaghetti serving spoon

Tips and Techniques for Cooking for One

When you are preparing meals just for yourself, it can seem like a lot of work at first. However, cooking for one doesn't have to be complicated, and over the years I've found great tips that can help you along the way. With a little planning and a few tricks up your sleeve, you'll find yourself open to a world of delicious, simple meals.

Tip 1: Plan Your Grocery Shopping

Plan your meals for the week to make preparing dishes for one much easier. When planning your meals, think about the different proteins or key ingredients you want to use and see how you can use them in more than one meal during the week. For example, you can roast a chicken or pork tenderloin in the oven on Sunday and use part of the protein for one meal on Monday and the remainder in other recipes later in the week. Do the same for ingredients like eggplant, peppers, and onions.

Tip 2: Shop Your Refrigerator and Pantry

Before you head to the store, look through your refrigerator and pantry. Take stock of what you already have so you don't purchase the same item again.

Also note what you may be running out of so you are not stuck when cooking during the next week.

Tip 3: Stock Up On Staples

Keep your pantry filled with canned beans, cans of diced tomatoes, rice, pasta, chicken broth, and spices. Dried or canned beans, dried lentils, and rice in particular keep for a very long time. Consider purchasing extra cans of beans when you find them on sale. You might also think about purchasing larger, often less expensive bags of rice to have on hand when you want to put a meal together quickly.

Tip 4: Shop the Bulk Bin Aisle

Many mainstream grocery stores and markets have a bulk bin aisle. Buying your spices from the bulk aisles can save you lots of money. And by measuring out exactly what you need and paying for a smaller amount, you will not be left with jars of partially used spices in your pantry. Purchasing spices this way also allows you to try a spice that you wouldn't normally buy. Also look for grains, pasta, and nuts in this aisle. Purchase the amount you need instead of larger packaged bags.

Tip 5: Experiment

Don't be afraid to experiment in the kitchen. Combining ingredients you love through trial and error is one of the easiest ways to learn how to cook—and enjoy doing it.

Tip 6: Ask to Purchase Meats, Cheeses, and Seafood in Smaller Quantities

Instead of buying prepackaged meat, cheese, or seafood, buy it from the meat, deli, or seafood counter. Ask to purchase the exact amount you need. If a particular cut of meat or type of seafood comes only in large packages, you can usually take it to the meat or seafood counter and ask them to repackage it into a smaller amount.

Tip 7: Visit the Salad Bars for Smaller Quantities

Often, you'll need only a small amount of olives, vegetables, or another ingredient for a recipe. No need to buy a large jar: Simply pick up the amount you need from the grocery store salad bar.

Tip 8: Make Weekends Your "Use It Up Weekend"

Try to use up all of the produce you might have left over from meals you made during the week. A veggie scramble is a delicious, filling breakfast, and can be made with extra peppers, mushrooms, and more. Leftover carrots, peas, and other vegetables can also be added to soups and pasta dishes. You can use any extra cheese you have for snacking, on sandwiches, shredded over scrambled eggs, cubed in salads, or stirred into pasta.

How to Avoid Wasting Food

Sometimes it's hard to know how much food to shop for when you're cooking for one. Many foods are packaged in large sizes, so when you need only a small amount, the remainder often gets tossed, either because you forget about it or don't know what to do with it. One way to make sure this does not happen is to meal plan. Spending even a few minutes every week planning meals for the week can save you a lot of time and money in the kitchen later. And that's not the only way to avoid wasting food! The following are simple tricks to ensure you use every last bit of what you buy:

- Freeze vegetables. Slice the entire onion, carrot, celery, or other vegetable, then transfer to small food storage bags. Label them, and put them in the freezer. Take a package out when you're ready to use it for soups, sauces, or other recipes.

- Purchase roasts, pork chops, ground beef, etc. when on sale. When you get home, divide them into individual portions, wrap twice with plastic wrap, and freeze in freezer bags. You can also divide bacon into single-serving portions by separating each slice of bacon and rolling it into a spiral. Place the spirals on a medium baking sheet and freeze them for at least 30 minutes until completely frozen. Put the frozen spirals in a freezer bag and keep them in the freezer until you are ready to use them.

- Shop farmers' markets and grocers for individual pieces of fruit or vegetables.

- Grow your own herbs in small containers at home. You can pick only what you need, and the plants will keep growing to provide more for later.

- Store flours and sugars in the freezer. They stay fresh longer when kept this way.

- Freeze sliced fruits such as melons and peaches. Store the fruit in single-serving food storage bags and use them in smoothies or as additions in your favorite recipes.

- Divide bread loaves in half. Keep one half at room temperature for use now, and freeze the rest.

- Make your own bread crumbs. Lightly toast your favorite bread, then tear it into large pieces and put the pieces in a blender or a food processor. Pulse until the bread has turned into crumbs. Store the bread crumbs in a jar or freezer bag until you are ready to use them.

Stocking Your Kitchen

A well-stocked kitchen allows you to create meals at the last minute with little or no planning. Once you have stocked your pantry and refrigerator with the things you use regularly, buying groceries is more about replenishing what you have used during the past week, as well as adding specific ingredients for meals you have planned for the coming days. If you are following a specific diet, it is also easier to keep to that diet by stocking up on the foods that fit within its restrictions, so you can avoid those midafternoon and late-night temptations.

The items found in the following list are the essentials that many recipes (including those in this book) are built on. Keep in mind that everyone's kitchen will look a little different; add or subtract items based on what you love and know you will use. You will be able to modify most of the recipes in this book to fit what you have:

Refrigerator
- Eggs
- Cheese
- Butter
- Heavy cream
- Plain yogurt
- Mayonnaise
- Mustard
- Carrots
- Bell peppers
- Celery
- Sausage (Italian and ground)
- Onions (red and yellow)
- Garlic
- Tomatoes (Roma and cherry)
- Lettuce (iceberg and romaine)
- Apples (red and green)
- Lemons
- Jams or jellies

Freezer
- Frozen chicken and fish
- Bread crumbs
- Frozen fruit

Pantry
- All-purpose flour
- Baking powder
- Baking soda
- Granulated sugar
- Powdered sugar
- Light and dark brown sugar
- Smooth peanut butter
- Bananas
- Canned beans (red, garbanzo, and black)
- Canned tomatoes (diced and whole)
- Pasta (small shaped, linguine, fettuccine, and spaghetti)
- Canned tuna
- Canned or boxed chicken and beef broth
- Vinegar (balsamic, red, white wine)
- Rice (brown and white)
- Tomato paste
- Extra-virgin olive oil
- Canola oil

Spices
- Kosher salt
- Ground black pepper
- Dried basil
- Italian seasoning
- Smoked paprika
- Cumin

How to Read a Recipe

It has been my experience that half of all recipes that "fail" do so because they were not completely followed. I know how it is: You get hungry and quickly thumb through the pages of a cookbook. When you discover an interesting recipe, you do a quick scan of the ingredients, and then start cooking immediately. Well, friends, that won't always work. It's important to slow down and read the recipe correctly.

Here's how:

- Read the recipe twice. Review the ingredient list and instructions carefully, and make notes if you have to. You want to fully understand the process ahead of you.

- Pay attention to the additional tips in sidebars. Sometimes there will be important tricks or advice in the sidebar that may change your recipe timeline. For example, "soak dry beans before cooking."

- Have all of the ingredients, dishes, and pans needed for the recipe close by and ready to use. Plan ahead for ingredient temperatures as well; for example, "1 large egg, room temperature" or "1 teaspoon butter, softened."

- Respect the order of ingredients. A recipe's ingredient list is usually set up by order of use.

- Pay attention to the comma. The comma is everything when it comes to recipe measurements. "½ cup all-purpose flour, sifted" is different than "½ cup sifted all-purpose flour." For "½ cup all-purpose flour, sifted," you would measure out the ½ cup of flour, and then sift it. For "½ cup sifted all-purpose flour," you would sift the flour and *then* measure out the ½ cup.

Is It Done Yet?

Doneness will typically be noted in a recipe by the amount of time that has passed and the appearance of the dish; for example, "bake 20 minutes until golden brown." Some ingredients will also give you clues as to their level of doneness via smell. For example, onions become fragrant when cooked. When cooking, be sure to use not only your oven timer, but also your eyes and your nose, as they can often tell you more than a timer ever will.

Simple Cooking for One

The food- and money-saving techniques in this chapter, paired with the delicious, healthy, and easy-to-follow recipes in the following pages, will set you up for success when cooking single and small-batch servings. Flip through these pages to choose the recipes you want to prepare, based on the items you've now stocked in your kitchen. This prep work will make cooking for one that much easier, so you can finally enjoy making and eating your meals. Let's get started.

CHAPTER TWO
BREAKFAST

You've always heard that breakfast is the most important meal of the day. *Breakfast* literally means "break the fast," and it gives you the energy you need to take on the day—so it's important that the first foods you ingest are healthy, satisfying ones, right? It's important to remember that breakfast for one doesn't have to be a hassle; with the right recipes in your arsenal, it can be a meal you look forward to preparing and enjoying.

In this chapter you'll find easy, delicious breakfast classics like the Denver Omelette, Blueberry Muffin, Waffle for One, and Buttermilk Biscuits, as well as filling grab-and-go recipes such as Fruit-Filled Overnight Oats, Strawberry Banana Smoothie, and Small-Batch Maple Nut Granola. You won't believe how simple—and fast—it can be to make a Strawberry-Filled Dutch Baby or Triple Chocolate Scones! Most of these recipes take just minutes to make, and any of them would be a great way to start your day.

MAPLE PECAN BREAKFAST BREAD PUDDING

SERVES 1 | PREP: 15 MINUTES | COOK: 30 MINUTES

 Bread pudding is a popular dessert that dates back to thirteenth-century England. Filled with crunchy pecans and pure maple syrup, it's not only ideal for breakfast but would make a lovely dessert as well!

INGREDIENTS

1 cup cubed French bread

1 tablespoon room temperature butter, divided

8 tablespoons heavy cream

1 large egg

2 tablespoons light brown sugar

½ tablespoon pure maple syrup

½ teaspoon vanilla extract

½ teaspoon granulated sugar

⅛ teaspoon ground cinnamon

2 tablespoons chopped pecans

1. Preheat oven to 350°F. Place cubed bread into a 5" × 5" baking dish coated with ½ tablespoon butter.

2. In a small bowl, whisk together cream, egg, brown sugar, maple syrup, and vanilla. Pour mixture over bread in pan.

3. In a separate small bowl, mix together granulated sugar and cinnamon. Sprinkle mixture over moistened bread and top with pecans.

4. Cut remaining ½ tablespoon butter into small bits and place evenly over top of bread.

5. Boil a kettle of water to make a water bath. Place baking dish with bread pudding into a larger 8" × 8" baking pan. Pour boiling water into larger pan until it reaches halfway up sides of bread pudding dish.

6. Place in oven and bake 30 minutes.

7. Carefully remove pans from oven. Remove baking dish from larger pan. Place on a rack to cool 5 minutes, then enjoy immediately.

What Is a Water Bath?

A water bath, or a *bain-marie*, is a dish of water used to bake recipes requiring gentle, even heat. It insulates the dish so that it doesn't overcook. All you need is a roasting pan large enough to accommodate the custard dish. The walls of the pans should not touch.

PER SERVING

Calories: 891
Fat: 71g
Protein: 14g
Sodium: 285mg

Fiber: 2g
Carbohydrates: 55g
Sugar: 37g

DENVER OMELETTE

SERVES 1 | PREP: 10 MINUTES | COOK: 10 MINUTES

 A Denver Omelette, also known as a "Western omelette" or "Southwest omelette," is filled with diced ham, onions, and bell peppers. This meal comes together quickly to make a wonderfully filling breakfast. Use either an 8" skillet for a thicker omelette, or a 10" skillet for a thinner, larger omelette.

INGREDIENTS

1 tablespoon room temperature butter

¼ cup diced cooked ham

2 tablespoons peeled and chopped yellow onion

2 tablespoons chopped green bell pepper

1 clove garlic, peeled and minced

⅛ teaspoon kosher salt

⅛ teaspoon freshly ground black pepper

3 large eggs, beaten

⅓ cup shredded Cheddar cheese

1. In an 8" skillet over medium heat, melt butter 30 seconds.
2. Add ham, onions, bell peppers, and garlic to pan. Sprinkle in salt and pepper, and cook until onions start to soften, about 5 minutes.
3. Pour eggs into skillet and tilt to coat, cooking ingredients evenly.
4. Sprinkle cheese evenly over eggs. Cook, tilting skillet occasionally, until top is slightly wet but not runny, about 3 minutes.
5. Using a spatula, fold omelette in half and transfer to a medium plate. Enjoy immediately.

PER SERVING

Calories: 530
Fat: 40g
Protein: 33g
Sodium: 1,184mg

Fiber: 1g
Carbohydrates: 8g
Sugar: 3g

SMALL-BATCH MAPLE NUT GRANOLA

YIELDS 1 CUP | PREP: 10 MINUTES | COOK: 30 MINUTES

 You simply can't beat the taste of homemade granola, and once you see just how easy it is to make, you'll never go back to the store-bought versions again. This Small-Batch Maple Nut Granola is perfectly sweet, crunchy, and wonderful served with milk or yogurt. Granola also makes a great snack. Keep a jar on hand to enjoy by the handfuls!

INGREDIENTS

1 tablespoon room temperature butter

2 tablespoons pure maple syrup

⅛ teaspoon kosher salt

¼ teaspoon vanilla extract

½ cup old-fashioned oats

¼ cup chopped walnuts

¼ cup chopped pecans

2 tablespoons unsweetened shredded coconut

2 tablespoons light brown sugar

⅛ teaspoon ground cinnamon

1. Preheat oven to 350°F.

2. In a small saucepan over medium heat, melt butter 30 seconds. Stir in maple syrup and salt. Remove from heat and stir in vanilla.

3. In a medium bowl, combine oats, walnuts, pecans, coconut, brown sugar, and cinnamon. Pour in syrup mixture and stir until all ingredients are well coated.

4. Pour mixture onto a large ungreased baking sheet and spread evenly across entire sheet.

5. Bake 30 minutes, stirring every 10 minutes to achieve an even color.

6. Remove from oven and set on a cooling rack to cool 20 minutes, then transfer to a small bowl or container. Store at room temperature up to 3 weeks.

Homemade Granola Tips

Feel free to substitute other nuts in place of the walnuts and pecans in this recipe. You can also substitute the coconut with raisins or other dried fruit. If using dried fruit, be sure to add it to the granola *after* the granola has baked. Do not bake the granola with the dried fruit, because the fruit will burn on the pan.

PER SERVING

Calories: 975
Fat: 60g
Protein: 15g
Sodium: 311mg

Fiber: 12g
Carbohydrates: 102g
Sugar: 54g

PANCAKES FOR ONE

SERVES 1 | PREP: 5 MINUTES | COOK: 10 MINUTES

 Have you ever found yourself craving a stack of soft, fluffy pancakes for breakfast but hesitated to make them because you'd be left with more than you could eat? If so, you'll love this easy pancake recipe. These pancakes taste great on their own, but are also perfect for add-ins like chocolate chips or mashed banana. Enjoy with your favorite toppings: butter, syrup, fruit, and more.

INGREDIENTS

1 cup all-purpose flour

1 teaspoon baking powder

½ tablespoon granulated sugar

½ teaspoon kosher salt

1 large egg, beaten

¾ cup 1% milk

1 tablespoon butter, melted, plus 1 teaspoon butter, softened, divided

1. In a large bowl, whisk together flour, baking powder, sugar, and salt.

2. In a separate large bowl, add egg and whisk in milk and melted butter.

3. Pour wet ingredients into dry ingredients and stir well.

4. Add softened butter to a large skillet or griddle over medium heat. Melt 30 seconds, then ladle about ¾ cup batter onto skillet to make a pancake. Cook until bubbles break the surface of pancake and the underside is golden brown, about 3 minutes.

5. Flip with a spatula and cook other side about 1 minute more until golden brown. Remove from the pan and place on a medium plate.

6. Repeat cooking until all batter is used up.

7. Enjoy immediately.

PER SERVING

Calories: 750

Fat: 23g

Protein: 26g

Sodium: 1,682mg

Fiber: 3g

Carbohydrates: 108g

Sugar: 12g

SMALL-BATCH CINNAMON SUGAR DONUTS

MAKES 6 DONUTS | PREP: 10 MINUTES | COOK: 5 MINUTES

 This wonderful recipe yields six mouth-watering donut holes—the perfect amount to satisfy any sweet craving. You'll want to use a deep pot or skillet when frying the donuts, and the oil should heat to 350°F. (Using a thermometer will help you keep track of the temperature.) Use a slotted spoon to remove the donut holes from the oil to ensure they are properly drained.

INGREDIENTS

3 cups canola oil for frying

½ cup all-purpose flour

5 tablespoons granulated sugar, divided

½ teaspoon baking soda

¾ teaspoon ground cinnamon, divided

¼ teaspoon kosher salt

⅛ teaspoon ground nutmeg

1 large egg yolk

¼ cup 1% milk

½ tablespoon butter, melted

1. Pour oil into a 10" skillet over medium heat. Heat oil to 350°F.

2. While oil is heating, prepare donut batter by whisking together flour, 2 tablespoons sugar, baking soda, ¼ teaspoon cinnamon, salt, and nutmeg in a medium bowl.

3. In a separate small bowl, whisk together egg yolk, milk, and melted butter.

4. Pour wet ingredients into dry ingredients and stir to combine.

5. Once oil is heated, use a cookie scoop or spoon to carefully drop balls of batter into oil.

6. Fry donut holes 2 minutes on each side until golden brown.

7. Remove donut holes from oil with a slotted spoon. Transfer to a large paper towel–lined plate to drain.

8. In a small bowl, stir together 3 tablespoons sugar and ½ teaspoon cinnamon.

9. Place warm donut holes into a paper or zip-top bag and pour cinnamon sugar inside bag. Seal bag and give it a few shakes to coat donut holes.

10. Alternatively, roll each donut hole in the cinnamon sugar mixture to coat. Enjoy warm.

PER SERVING (1 DONUT)

Calories: 124   *Fiber: 0g*
Fat: 4g   *Carbohydrates: 19g*
Protein: 2g   *Sugar: 11g*
Sodium: 208mg

LEMON BLUEBERRY SCONES

MAKES 4 SCONES | PREP: 10 MINUTES | COOK: 20 MINUTES

 These buttery, melt-in-your-mouth Lemon Blueberry Scones are perfect to enjoy with a cup of coffee or tea. You can add in chopped walnuts for a little extra texture, or swap out the blueberries for raspberries or blackberries if you prefer! Scones will keep well in the refrigerator for two to three days.

INGREDIENTS

For Scones:

1 cup all-purpose flour

2 tablespoons granulated sugar

1 teaspoon baking powder

¼ teaspoon kosher salt

⅛ teaspoon baking soda

4 tablespoons (½ stick) cold butter, cut into small pieces

¼ cup 1% milk

1 large egg yolk

1 tablespoon lemon juice

1 tablespoon lemon zest

½ cup fresh blueberries

For Glaze

½ cup powdered sugar, sifted

1 tablespoon heavy cream

1 tablespoon lemon juice

1. **To make Scones:** Preheat oven to 425°F. Line a large baking sheet with parchment paper.

2. In a large mixing bowl, stir together flour, sugar, baking powder, salt, and baking soda.

3. Using a pastry blender, a fork, or your fingertips, cut butter into flour mixture until mixture resembles fine crumbs.

4. In a small bowl, whisk together milk, egg yolk, lemon juice, and lemon zest. Pour into flour mixture and stir until just combined.

5. Gently stir in blueberries.

6. Turn dough out onto a lightly floured work surface. Knead very lightly and form a 5" × 5" circle that is 1" thick.

7. Cut circle into four wedges and place on prepared baking sheet. Bake 13 minutes until golden brown.

8. Let cool on baking sheet for 5 minutes, then transfer onto a wire rack to cool completely, about 20 minutes.

1. **To make Glaze:** In a small bowl, whisk together powdered sugar, cream, and lemon juice until smooth. Spoon over cooled scones. Enjoy.

PER SERVING (1 SCONE)

Calories: 345   Fiber: 2g
Fat: 15g   Carbohydrates: 50g
Protein: 5g   Sugar: 24g
Sodium: 288mg

BUTTERMILK BISCUITS

MAKES 4 BISCUITS | PREP: 5 MINUTES | COOK: 12 MINUTES

 These drop biscuits are made with buttermilk, which helps to create a tender, buttery biscuit. For perfect biscuits it's important to make sure your butter is cold and to not overmix the dough. Ready in 20 minutes, these biscuits are perfect for breakfast, or with a bowl of soup or stew.

INGREDIENTS

1 cup all-purpose flour

1 teaspoon baking powder

1 teaspoon granulated sugar

½ teaspoon kosher salt

3 tablespoons cold butter, cut into ¼" pieces

½ cup plus 2 tablespoons buttermilk

1. Preheat oven to 400°F and line a large baking sheet with parchment paper.

2. In a large bowl, whisk together flour, baking powder, sugar, and salt.

3. Using a pastry blender, a fork, or your fingertips, cut butter into flour mixture until it resembles coarse sand. Add buttermilk and stir just until dough comes together.

4. Using a large spoon, drop four spoonfuls of batter on baking sheet and bake until golden brown, about 10 minutes. Enjoy.

Making a Substitute for Buttermilk

If you don't have buttermilk, you can make your own by mixing ½ cup whole milk with ½ tablespoon lemon juice or white vinegar. Let sit for 10 minutes at room temperature before using.

PER SERVING (1 BISCUIT)

Calories: 218

Fat: 40g

Protein: 5g

Sodium: 423mg

Fiber: 1g

Carbohydrates: 27g

Sugar: 3g

CHEESY BAKED EGGS

These Cheesy Baked Eggs are a great way to start the day! They are low carb, and can be ready in under 20 minutes. Add a pinch of paprika for a little kick.

INGREDIENTS

1 teaspoon butter, softened

2 large eggs

2 tablespoons heavy cream

2 tablespoons shredded Cheddar cheese

1 tablespoon grated Parmesan cheese

⅛ teaspoon kosher salt

⅛ teaspoon freshly ground black pepper

1. Preheat oven to 400°F. Coat inside of an 8-ounce oven-safe ramekin with butter.
2. In a small bowl, whisk together eggs and cream.
3. Stir in cheeses, salt, and pepper.
4. Pour mixture into ramekin and bake 16 minutes or until eggs are set. Enjoy immediately.

PER SERVING

Calories: 357 | Fat: 30g | Protein: 19g | Sodium: 618mg
Fiber: 0g | Carbohydrates: 2g | Sugar: 1g

FRUIT-FILLED OVERNIGHT OATS

The idea is to soak rolled oats in a liquid overnight so they soften. When the oats are combined with spices and fruit, the outcome is simply heavenly. The best part of this breakfast recipe is that it is easily customizable. It calls for blueberries, but you can use any of your favorite fresh fruits, as well as chopped walnuts, almonds, and more.

INGREDIENTS

½ cup old-fashioned oats

½ cup plain almond milk

¼ cup plain full-fat yogurt

¼ cup fresh blueberries

⅛ teaspoon ground nutmeg

1 teaspoon pure honey

1. Add the oats to a large glass jar. Pour in milk, then add remaining ingredients.
2. Cover jar and refrigerate overnight.
3. In the morning, stir and enjoy.

PER SERVING

Calories: 315 | Fat: 7g | Protein: 10g | Sodium: 124mg
Fiber: 7g | Carbohydrates: 53g | Sugar: 12g

WAFFLE FOR ONE

SERVES 1 | PREP: 5 MINUTES | COOK: 10 MINUTES

 There's nothing better than homemade waffles in the morning. This easy recipe delivers one delightful, fluffy waffle with a perfectly crisp exterior and soft and tender insides. It's fantastic topped with butter and syrup for breakfast, or as a dessert topped with whipped cream and chocolate syrup. Depending on the size of your waffle maker, you might have a bit of extra batter left over. If so, use it to make a second, smaller waffle.

INGREDIENTS

1 large egg, beaten

½ cup 1% milk

¼ teaspoon vanilla extract

1 tablespoon butter, melted

1 tablespoon granulated sugar

½ cup all-purpose flour

½ teaspoon baking powder

⅛ teaspoon kosher salt

1. Preheat waffle iron. Spray with nonstick cooking spray or brush with melted butter.

2. In a large bowl, mix egg with milk, vanilla, melted butter, and sugar.

3. Whisk in flour, baking powder, and salt and mix gently until combined. Do not overmix.

4. Pour batter onto iron, close lid, and cook 5 minutes.

5. Use a pair of tongs to transfer waffle to a medium plate and enjoy immediately.

PER SERVING

Calories: 505
Fat: 18g
Protein: 17g
Sodium: 600mg

Fiber: 2g
Carbohydrates: 67g
Sugar: 19g

STRAWBERRY-FILLED DUTCH BABY

SERVES 1 | PREP: 5 MINUTES | COOK: 20 MINUTES

 This Strawberry-Filled Dutch Baby is perfect for breakfast or even dessert. Also called a Puffed Pancake, it is a cross between a pancake and a crepe. Filled with sweet strawberries, it is typically baked in a 6.5" skillet, but can also be baked in a 5" × 5" baking dish. Enjoy it with a dusting of powdered sugar.

INGREDIENTS

½ tablespoon cold butter

1 large egg

¼ cup 1% milk

½ teaspoon vanilla extract

1 teaspoon granulated sugar

¼ cup all-purpose flour

⅛ teaspoon kosher salt

¼ cup sliced fresh strawberries

1. Preheat oven to 400°F.

2. Put butter in a 6.5" cast-iron skillet or oven-safe baking dish and place in oven.

3. In a small bowl, whisk together egg, milk, vanilla, and sugar. Add flour and salt and whisk vigorously to remove lumps. Set aside.

4. Using oven mitts, carefully remove skillet from oven. Swirl butter around in skillet to coat completely.

5. Add strawberries to skillet, then pour batter over strawberries.

6. Place skillet back in oven and cook until batter is puffed in the center and golden brown along the edges, about 20 minutes.

7. Remove from oven and use a spatula to transfer Dutch Baby from skillet to a cooling rack or medium plate to cool 10 minutes. Enjoy.

What Is a Dutch Baby?

A Dutch Baby begins with a thin, pancake-like batter that is poured into a hot skillet and put in the oven. The batter will start to rise and puff up, and when the edges begin to brown, it is ready to come out of the oven. When the Dutch Baby has the chance to cool slightly, the puff collapses into the pan, and what remains is a pancake with the texture of a delicate crepe.

PER SERVING

Calories: 297
Fat: 12g
Protein: 12g
Sodium: 391mg

Fiber: 2g
Carbohydrates: 35g
Sugar: 10g

HAM AND CHEESE CRUSTLESS QUICHE

SERVES 1 | PREP: 10 MINUTES | COOK: 25 MINUTES

Crustless quiche is a high-protein meal that is perfect for breakfast, lunch, or dinner and is so incredibly tasty, you won't even miss the crust!

INGREDIENTS

2 large eggs

4 tablespoons heavy cream

¼ teaspoon kosher salt

⅛ teaspoon freshly ground black pepper

⅛ teaspoon ground nutmeg

⅓ cup (about 2 ounces) diced ham

½ cup (about 4 ounces) shredded Cheddar cheese

1. Preheat oven to 375°F.

2. In a medium bowl, whisk together eggs and cream. Stir in salt, pepper, nutmeg, ham, and cheese.

3. Pour mixture into a 5" × 5" baking dish lightly greased with butter or oil.

4. Bake dish 25 minutes, until quiche is puffed and golden.

Basic Crustless Quiche Recipe

A single-serving crustless quiche begins with two ingredients: 2 eggs and 4 tablespoons of cream. From there, begin to experiment with different proteins and cheeses. Just keep the amounts of meats and cheeses you use the same as in this recipe.

PER SERVING

Calories: 876   Fiber: 0g
Fat: 71g   Carbohydrates: 10g
Protein: 49g   Sugar: 4g
Sodium: 2,188mg

OVERNIGHT FRENCH TOAST CASSEROLE WITH STREUSEL TOPPING

SERVES 1 | PREP: 10 MINUTES | COOK: 30 MINUTES

 This small-batch French toast casserole comes together the night before you want to enjoy it! You won't find it to be extremely sweet, as most people like to add their own toppings like syrup and/or a sprinkle of sugar.

INGREDIENTS

For French Toast

4½"-thick slices French bread

1 large egg

¼ cup heavy cream

½ cup 1% milk

2 teaspoons granulated sugar

¼ teaspoon vanilla extract

⅛ teaspoon ground cinnamon

⅛ teaspoon ground nutmeg

⅛ teaspoon kosher salt

For Topping

2 tablespoons butter, softened

2 teaspoons light brown sugar

⅛ teaspoon ground cinnamon

⅛ teaspoon ground nutmeg

1 tablespoon chopped pecans

1. Arrange slices of French bread in a 5" × 5" baking dish greased with butter or oil. (Slices can be overlapped.)

2. In a small bowl, whisk together egg, cream, milk, sugar, vanilla, cinnamon, nutmeg, and salt.

3. Pour mixture over bread slices, making sure all slices are covered evenly. Cover and refrigerate overnight.

4. When ready to serve, preheat oven to 350°F.

5. Combine topping ingredients in a small bowl. Spread evenly over bread and bake 32 minutes until puffed and lightly golden.

6. Remove from oven and enjoy.

PER SERVING

Calories: 1,696   *Fiber: 10g*
Fat: 65g   *Carbohydrates: 227g*
Protein: 54g   *Sugar: 43g*
Sodium: 2,749mg

CINNAMON COFFEE CAKE WITH STREUSEL TOPPING

SERVES 1 | PREP: 10 MINUTES | COOK: 40 MINUTES

 Coffee cakes are the perfect excuse for eating cake at any time of the day. This buttery, streusel-topped coffee cake would go extremely well with your morning coffee, but would also satisfy an afternoon sweet craving.

INGREDIENTS

For Coffee Cake

2 tablespoons butter, melted

5 tablespoons granulated sugar

1 large egg yolk

¼ teaspoon vanilla extract

5 tablespoons all-purpose flour

⅛ teaspoon baking powder

¼ teaspoon ground cinnamon

⅛ teaspoon kosher salt

2 tablespoons 1% milk

For Streusel Topping

2 tablespoons light brown sugar

½ teaspoon granulated sugar

¼ teaspoon ground cinnamon

2 tablespoons all-purpose flour

1 tablespoon butter, softened

1. **To make Coffee Cake:** Preheat oven to 350°F.

2. In a small bowl, stir together butter and sugar until well blended. Add in egg yolk and vanilla and stir until combined.

3. In a separate small bowl, whisk together flour, baking powder, cinnamon, and salt. Pour into egg mixture and stir to combine.

4. Stir in milk and pour mixture into an 8-ounce ramekin lightly greased with butter or oil.

1. **To make Streusel Topping:** Use a fork to mix together all ingredients in a small bowl until crumbly. Spoon evenly over coffee cake batter.

2. Bake 40 minutes or until top is golden brown. Cake is cooked through if a sharp knife inserted in the center comes out clean. Enjoy warm.

PER SERVING

Calories: 935
Fat: 40g
Protein: 10g
Sodium: 372mg

Fiber: 2g
Carbohydrates: 137g
Sugar: 94g

BLUEBERRY MUFFIN

SERVES 1 | PREP: 10 MINUTES | COOK: 15 MINUTES

 This big, bakery-style Blueberry Muffin is loaded with plump, sweet blueberries and can be baked in an 8- or 10-ounce ramekin. Feel free to use frozen blueberries if fresh ones aren't in season, and top your muffin with a pat of butter.

INGREDIENTS

½ cup all-purpose flour

½ teaspoon baking powder

⅛ teaspoon kosher salt

2 tablespoons butter, melted

3 tablespoons granulated sugar

1 large egg yolk

½ teaspoon vanilla extract

4 tablespoons 1% milk

½ cup fresh blueberries

1. Preheat oven to 400°F.

2. In a small bowl, mix together flour, baking powder, and salt. Set aside.

3. In a separate medium bowl, stir together melted butter and sugar. Add egg yolk, vanilla, and milk and whisk until completely blended.

4. Stir wet ingredients into dry ingredients and gently fold in blueberries. Pour into an 8-ounce ramekin greased with butter or oil.

5. Bake 15 minutes or until top is golden and center is completely cooked.

6. Remove ramekin from oven and place on a rack to cool slightly, about 15 minutes. Enjoy while still warm.

PER SERVING

Calories: 561

Fat: 29g

Protein: 12g

Sodium: 513mg

Fiber: 3g

Carbohydrates: 63g

Sugar: 11g

QUICHE-STUFFED PEPPER

SERVES 1 | PREP: 10 MINUTES | COOK: 40 MINUTES

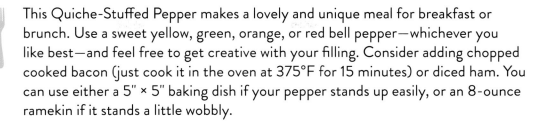

This Quiche-Stuffed Pepper makes a lovely and unique meal for breakfast or brunch. Use a sweet yellow, green, orange, or red bell pepper—whichever you like best—and feel free to get creative with your filling. Consider adding chopped cooked bacon (just cook it in the oven at 375°F for 15 minutes) or diced ham. You can use either a 5" × 5" baking dish if your pepper stands up easily, or an 8-ounce ramekin if it stands a little wobbly.

INGREDIENTS

1 medium green bell pepper, top removed, seeded, and cut in half

½ tablespoon olive oil

¼ cup peeled and chopped yellow onion

1 clove garlic, peeled and minced

¼ cup (about 2 ounces) fresh baby spinach, loosely packed

1 large egg

2 tablespoons heavy cream

⅛ teaspoon kosher salt

⅛ teaspoon freshly ground black pepper

2 tablespoons shredded Cheddar cheese

1. Preheat oven to 375°F. Lightly butter either a 5" × 5" baking dish or 8-ounce ramekin. Set aside.

2. Place pepper halves in baking dish or ramekin. Set aside.

3. In an 8" skillet over medium-high heat, cook oil 30 seconds. Add onions and garlic and cook, stirring occasionally, until onions are soft and translucent, about 2 minutes.

4. Add spinach and cook, stirring constantly, until spinach has wilted, about 1 minute. Remove skillet from heat and set aside.

5. In a medium bowl, whisk together egg, cream, salt, and pepper. Stir in cooked onion mixture and cheese.

6. Pour mixture into pepper halves and bake 40 minutes until center is cooked.

7. Remove from the oven and enjoy immediately.

PER SERVING

Calories: 361
Fat: 27g
Protein: 14g
Sodium: 512mg
Fiber: 4g
Carbohydrates: 16g
Sugar: 8g

OVERNIGHT BREAKFAST CASSEROLE

SERVES 1 | PREP: 12 MINUTES | COOK: 30 MINUTES

 This single-serving breakfast casserole is inspired by the legendary recipe my mother made every Christmas Eve when I was growing up! Feel free to substitute any of your favorite meats, or add in vegetables such as bell pepper and onion.

INGREDIENTS

6 ounces pork sausage

1 large egg, beaten

¾ cup 1% milk

⅛ teaspoon kosher salt

⅛ teaspoon freshly ground black pepper

2 cups cubed French bread

½ cup shredded Cheddar cheese

1. In a medium skillet greased with butter or oil, cook sausage over medium heat until no longer pink, about 6 minutes.

2. Once done, transfer sausage to a paper towel–lined plate and set aside.

3. In a small bowl, whisk egg together with milk, salt, and pepper. Set aside.

4. Grease a 5" × 5" baking dish with butter or oil. Line dish with bread.

5. Top bread with cooked sausage and cheese. Pour egg mixture over dish. Cover with aluminum foil and refrigerate overnight.

6. When ready to serve, preheat oven to 350°F.

7. Cook casserole, still covered, 25 minutes or until egg mixture is set.

8. Remove from oven and enjoy while hot.

PER SERVING

Calories: 862
Fat: 51g
Protein: 48g
Sodium: 1,799mg

Fiber: 2g
Carbohydrates: 50g
Sugar: 15g

TRIPLE CHOCOLATE SCONES

 MAKES 4 SCONES | **PREP: 10 MINUTES** | **COOK: 15 MINUTES**

These Triple Chocolate Scones are a chocolate lover's dream! They will keep well in the refrigerator for up to three days.

INGREDIENTS

For Scones

1 cup all-purpose flour

2 tablespoons unsweetened cocoa powder

2½ tablespoons granulated sugar

1 teaspoon baking powder

¼ teaspoon kosher salt

⅛ teaspoon baking soda

⅛ teaspoon ground cinnamon

¼ cup (½ stick) cold butter, cut into pieces

1 large egg yolk

¼ cup whole milk

½ teaspoon vanilla extract

½ cup semi-sweet chocolate chips

For Chocolate Glaze

½ cup powdered sugar

1½ tablespoons brewed coffee, cooled

4 tablespoons semi-sweet chocolate chips, melted

PER SERVING (1 SCONE)

Calories: 279	Fiber: 2g
Fat: 14g	Carbohydrates: 35g
Protein: 5g	Sugar: 9g
Sodium: 287mg	

1. **To make Scones:** Preheat oven to 400°F. Line a large baking sheet with parchment paper.

2. In a large mixing bowl, stir together flour, cocoa powder, sugar, baking powder, salt, baking soda, and cinnamon.

3. Using a pastry blender, a fork, or your fingertips, cut butter into flour mixture until it resembles fine crumbs.

4. In a separate small bowl, whisk together egg yolk, milk, and vanilla.

5. Pour egg mixture into flour mixture and stir until just combined. Gently fold in chocolate chips.

6. Turn dough out onto a lightly floured work surface. Knead very lightly to form a 5" × 5" circle that is about 1" thick. (Add a little more flour to dough if it becomes too sticky to handle.)

7. Cut dough into four triangle wedges and place on baking sheet. Bake 12 minutes until a toothpick inserted in the center of each scone comes out clean.

8. Remove from oven and let cool on baking sheet 5 minutes, then transfer to a wire rack to continue cooling, about 15 minutes.

1. **To make Glaze:** In a small bowl, whisk together powdered sugar, coffee, and melted chocolate until smooth. Add extra powdered sugar if the glaze appears to be too thin, or add extra coffee if the glaze is too thick. Spoon glaze over cooled scones and enjoy.

STRAWBERRY BANANA SMOOTHIE

SERVES 1 | PREP: 5 MINUTES | COOK: 0 MINUTES

Smoothies are a tasty, energizing breakfast. Feel free to use almond or soy milk instead of cow's milk in this recipe. If the smoothie is too thick, add more milk. If it is too thin, add more fruit or ice. Easy, delicious, and good for you too!

INGREDIENTS

1 large banana, peeled

½ cup frozen strawberries

1 cup 1% milk

¼ cup low-fat vanilla yogurt

1 tablespoon pure honey

1. Add all ingredients to a blender, place lid on blender, and pulse until combined.

2. Pour into a large glass and enjoy immediately.

PER SERVING

Calories: 365 | Fat: 4g | Protein: 13g | Sodium: 151mg
Fiber: 5g | Carbohydrates: 76g | Sugar: 58g

MANGO OAT BREAKFAST SMOOTHIE

SERVES 1 | PREP: 5 MINUTES | COOK: 0 MINUTES

This naturally sweetened smoothie is perfect for breakfast but also makes an ideal midday snack. Oats are incredibly nutritious and a powerful source of fiber; you'll love this nontraditional way of incorporating them into your breakfast routine.

INGREDIENTS

1 cup plain almond milk

¼ cup low-fat vanilla yogurt

1 large banana, peeled and sliced into large chunks

2 tablespoons quick-cooking oats

½ cup frozen mango chunks

⅛ teaspoon ground cinnamon

1. Add all ingredients to a blender, place lid on blender, and pulse until combined.

2. Pour into a large glass and enjoy immediately.

PER SERVING

Calories: 315 | Fat: 5g | Protein: 8g | Sodium: 269mg
Fiber: 6g | Carbohydrates: 64g | Sugar: 39g

FRUIT-FILLED BAKED OATMEAL

SERVES 1 | PREP: 10 MINUTES | COOK: 40 MINUTES

 Oats are always a wonderful choice for breakfast, and this baked oatmeal gives you a new way to enjoy them. Eat hot, served with milk, yogurt, or cream, drizzled with additional honey, or as is. You can also substitute the blueberries for your favorite fruits. Sliced bananas, sliced strawberries, and chopped apples are wonderful additions.

INGREDIENTS

1 tablespoon butter, melted and divided

¼ cup old-fashioned oats

⅛ teaspoon ground cinnamon

⅛ teaspoon kosher salt

¼ cup 1% milk

¼ teaspoon vanilla extract

1 tablespoon pure honey

1 large egg

¼ cup fresh blueberries

1. Preheat oven to 350°F. Generously grease a 5" × 5" baking dish with ½ tablespoon butter.

2. In a small bowl, mix together oats, cinnamon, and salt. Set aside.

3. In a separate small bowl, whisk together milk, ½ tablespoon butter, vanilla, honey, and egg.

4. Arrange blueberries in a single layer in bottom of prepared baking dish. Sprinkle oat mixture over fruit, then pour wet ingredients over top.

5. Bake until top is golden brown, about 40 minutes. Enjoy.

PER SERVING

Calories: 366
Fat: 18g
Protein: 10g
Sodium: 366mg

Fiber: 4g
Carbohydrates: 42g
Sugar: 21g

EGG AND MUFFIN SANDWICH

SERVES 1 | PREP: 3 MINUTES | COOK: 1 MINUTE

 This light egg sandwich is ready in less than 5 minutes! While the English muffin is toasting, the egg cooks in the microwave. This recipe uses American cheese, but you can substitute with your own favorite type.

INGREDIENTS

1 large egg

1 tablespoon water

1 English muffin

½ tablespoon room temperature butter

1 slice American cheese

1 thick slice deli ham

1. Grease the inside of a small bowl or coffee mug with cooking spray. Add egg and water and mix with a fork until combined.

2. Microwave on high 30 seconds, then stir. Microwave another 30 seconds until egg is almost set.

3. Toast English muffin in a toaster, then butter both sides. Place cooked egg on bottom half. Top with cheese, ham, and second half of English muffin. Enjoy immediately.

How to Store Leftover English Muffins

If you have English muffins or a loaf of bread that you don't see yourself using anytime soon, wrap them tightly in plastic wrap (to prevent freezer burn) and store them in the freezer until you are ready to use them.

PER SERVING

Calories: 370   Fiber: 2g
Fat: 18g   Carbohydrates: 29g
Protein: 20g   Sugar: 3g
Sodium: 858mg

MICROWAVE HAM AND SWISS SCRAMBLED EGGS

SERVES 1 | PREP: 1 MINUTE | COOK: 1 MINUTE

 There's no excuse to skip breakfast when you can have light and fluffy scrambled eggs with ham and cheese in just one minute. Feel free to substitute other types of cheese such as Cheddar or Gruyère for the Swiss. Breakfast couldn't be easier!

INGREDIENTS

1 thin slice deli ham, chopped

1 large egg, beaten

1 tablespoon shredded Cheddar cheese

1. Grease an 8-ounce ramekin or large coffee mug with cooking spray. Add ham, egg, and cheese.

2. Microwave on high 30 seconds, then stir.

3. Microwave again for 30 seconds until egg is cooked through. Enjoy warm.

PER SERVING

Calories: 146
Fat: 10g
Protein: 13g
Sodium: 437mg

Fiber: 0g
Carbohydrates: 2g
Sugar: 0g

BANANAS FOSTER OATMEAL

SERVES 1 | PREP: 5 MINUTES | COOK: 25 MINUTES

 Bananas Foster is a decadent treat made with bananas, brown sugar, and rum sauce, and is typically served with vanilla ice cream. Although perfect for dessert, it can be even better for breakfast! In this recipe I've eliminated the rum, but feel free to add an ⅛ teaspoon rum extract to the sauce.

INGREDIENTS

½ cup water

⅓ cup 1% milk

⅛ teaspoon kosher salt

½ cup old-fashioned oats

2 tablespoons room temperature butter, cubed

2 tablespoons packed light brown sugar

⅛ teaspoon ground cinnamon

⅛ teaspoon ground ginger

⅛ teaspoon ground nutmeg

1 medium ripe banana, peeled and sliced

⅛ teaspoon vanilla extract

1. In a 1-quart saucepan over high heat, bring water, milk, and salt to a boil.

2. Stir in oats and turn heat down to medium. Cook 5 minutes, stirring occasionally. Once done, remove from heat, cover, and set aside.

3. In an 8" skillet, melt butter over medium heat 30 seconds. Stir in brown sugar and spices and bring to a boil. Once boiling, reduce heat to low and simmer uncovered 5 minutes until slightly thickened.

4. Add sliced bananas and cook, stirring gently, 2 minutes until bananas are glazed and slightly softened. Remove from heat and stir in vanilla.

5. Stir banana mixture into oatmeal and transfer to a medium bowl. Enjoy while hot.

PER SERVING

Calories: 666   Fiber: 9g
Fat: 28g   Carbohydrates: 97g
Protein: 11g   Sugar: 45g
Sodium: 341mg

SAUSAGE AND PEPPER FRITTATA

SERVES 1 | PREP: 10 MINUTES | COOK: 20 MINUTES

 A frittata is a wonderful meal to make when you have a bunch of leftover ingredients in your refrigerator. In this case, I've combined spicy sausage with sweet red peppers, onions, and cheese. The frittata is baked in a 6.5" cast-iron skillet, but you can use any oven-safe pan or baking dish of a similar size.

INGREDIENTS

½ teaspoon olive oil

2 ounces Italian sausage

½ cup peeled and chopped yellow onion

½ cup chopped red peppers

2 large eggs

2 tablespoons heavy cream

¼ teaspoon dried thyme

⅛ teaspoon kosher salt

⅛ teaspoon freshly ground black pepper

½ cup shredded Cheddar cheese

1. In a 6.5" cast-iron skillet over medium-high heat, heat oil 30 seconds. Add sausage and sauté until lightly browned, about 3 minutes.

2. Add chopped onions and peppers and sauté until vegetables are soft, about 5 minutes.

3. Heat broiler to low. Meanwhile, whisk together eggs, cream, thyme, salt, and pepper in a medium bowl.

4. Stir in cheese and pour mixture into skillet with sausage and vegetables. Cook until eggs are set on bottom but top remains slightly runny, about 5 minutes.

5. Transfer skillet to oven and broil until eggs are set, about 3 minutes. Enjoy.

PER SERVING

Calories: 804

Fat: 64g

Protein: 39g

Sodium: 1,237mg

Fiber: 3g

Carbohydrates: 18g

Sugar: 9g

CHAPTER THREE
SIDE DISHES

Side dishes often remain in the shadows while the main dish steals the spotlight, but actually, side dishes can make the whole meal. Just think of Thanksgiving dinner without the mashed potatoes or cranberry sauce. Is a burger as appealing without the steak fries? I think not. Of course, it can be difficult to think of what to serve as a side, and you may feel tempted to forgo any altogether, assuming it will mean a lot of extra time spent in the kitchen when you just want to get to the eating part. Luckily, this doesn't have to be the case!

This chapter offers dozens of side dish recipes that are not only easy to make, but are also incredibly delicious. From favorites such as Mashed Potatoes and Corn Bread, to traditional holiday sides such as Sweet Potato Casserole and Sausage Pine Nut Dressing, to unique takes on the side salad like Spinach Orzo Salad, you'll discover single-serving recipes that will go well with any meal. You can even make a side dish as a standalone snack or small meal if you aren't as hungry. So let's dig in!

CORN BREAD

SERVES 1 | PREP: 10 MINUTES | COOK: 20 MINUTES

 This single-serving recipe delivers a slightly crumbly, perfectly sweet and buttery Corn Bread. It can be baked in a 6.5" cast-iron skillet or similar-sized baking dish. It is the perfect side for soups and stews and is so tasty you'll want to eat it all in one sitting.

INGREDIENTS

2½ tablespoons butter, melted

¼ cup 1% milk

1 large egg

¼ cup plus 1 tablespoon yellow cornmeal

¼ cup all-purpose flour

2 tablespoons granulated sugar

¼ teaspoon baking powder

¼ teaspoon kosher salt

1. Preheat oven to 400°F.

2. In a medium bowl, whisk together melted butter, milk, and egg.

3. In a separate medium bowl, mix together cornmeal, flour, sugar, baking powder, and salt.

4. Add cornmeal mixture to milk mixture and stir just until flour is moistened.

5. Pour batter into a 6.5" cast-iron skillet greased with oil or butter and spread evenly.

6. Bake 22 minutes until top is golden brown and a toothpick inserted in the center comes out clean. Enjoy warm.

PER SERVING

Calories: 587
Fat: 35g
Protein: 11g
Sodium: 787mg

Fiber: 6g
Carbohydrates: 58g
Sugar: 28g

ROASTED GARLIC CAULIFLOWER

SERVES 1 | PREP: 5 MINUTES | COOK: 20 MINUTES

 If you've roasted vegetables before then you know how incredibly easy and unbelievably flavorful they are. For this simple recipe you'll toss cauliflower florets in a little bit of olive oil and garlic and season them with salt and pepper. Feel free to add in other spices you like, such as dried basil or ground turmeric.

INGREDIENTS

1 cup (about 6 ounces) cauliflower florets

2 cloves garlic, peeled and sliced in half lengthwise

½ tablespoon olive oil

⅛ teaspoon kosher salt

⅛ teaspoon freshly ground black pepper

2 tablespoons grated Parmesan cheese

1. Preheat oven to 425°F.

2. Place cauliflower and garlic in a medium bowl. Drizzle with oil, sprinkle with salt and pepper, and toss to combine.

3. Transfer cauliflower and garlic onto a small rimmed (ungreased) baking sheet or small baking dish and spread into an even layer.

4. Roast until golden brown and tender, about 22 minutes.

5. Transfer to a medium plate, top with Parmesan, and enjoy warm.

Tips for Roasting Vegetables
Roast vegetables at 425°F for best results. Also, cut them into evenly sized pieces so that they cook for the same amount of time, and do not overcrowd them in the roasting pan. (This method works wonderfully with carrots, broccoli, butternut squash, and cauliflower.)

PER SERVING

Calories: 153
Fat: 10g
Protein: 7g
Sodium: 513mg

Fiber: 4g
Carbohydrates: 11g
Sugar: 3g

OVEN-ROASTED POTATOES

SERVES 1 | PREP: 5 MINUTES | COOK: 30 MINUTES

These Oven-Roasted Potatoes are the perfect side dish to enjoy with meat, chicken, or fish. When roasted, the skins of potatoes become crispy, while the insides are soft and creamy. It's hard to resist eating these potatoes straight from the baking sheet!

INGREDIENTS

½ pound baby red potatoes, scrubbed and sliced into bite-sized pieces

½ tablespoon olive oil

¼ teaspoon dried rosemary

⅛ teaspoon kosher salt

⅛ teaspoon freshly ground black pepper

1. Preheat oven to 425°F.
2. Add potatoes to a medium bowl and toss with oil, rosemary, salt, and pepper.
3. Spread potatoes out onto a large ungreased baking sheet. Bake 25 minutes until tender. Enjoy while hot.

PER SERVING

Calories: 220 | Fat: 7g | Protein: 4g | Sodium: 332mg Fiber: 4g | Carbohydrates: 36g | Sugar: 3g

ROASTED BROCCOLI

SERVES 1 | PREP: 5 MINUTES | COOK: 25 MINUTES

This Roasted Broccoli is so easy to make and is the perfect side dish to complement any entrée. One broccoli crown is an ideal amount to use when you are cooking for one. Elevate this dish by adding a little shaved Parmesan cheese to the broccoli as soon as you take it out of the oven.

INGREDIENTS

¼ pound broccoli florets (about 1 broccoli crown)

1 tablespoon olive oil

⅛ teaspoon kosher salt

⅛ teaspoon freshly ground black pepper

⅛ teaspoon garlic powder

1. Preheat oven to 425°F.
2. Scatter broccoli on a small ungreased rimmed baking sheet. Drizzle oil over broccoli and season with salt, pepper, and garlic powder. Toss until florets are evenly coated.
3. Roast for 22 minutes, until cooked and slightly browned. Remove from oven and enjoy warm.

PER SERVING

Calories: 126 | Fat: 14g | Protein: 1g | Sodium: 296mg Fiber: 1g | Carbohydrates: 1g | Sugar: 0g

HONEY-ROASTED CARROTS

SERVES 1 | PREP: 5 MINUTES | COOK: 25 MINUTES

 This Honey-Roasted Carrots recipe features two carrots sliced and seasoned with a touch of salt and pepper, then bathed in butter and honey. It's an easy yet elegant side dish that takes minutes to prepare. Enjoy alongside your favorite chicken, pork, or vegetarian entrée.

INGREDIENTS

2 large carrots, peeled and sliced into 2"-long sections

1 tablespoon olive oil

1 tablespoon pure honey

¼ teaspoon kosher salt

⅛ teaspoon freshly ground black pepper

½ tablespoon butter, melted

1. Preheat oven to 400°F. Spread carrots on a large foil-lined baking sheet.

2. In a small bowl, mix together oil, honey, salt, and pepper. Pour mixture over carrots and use your hand to toss until coated.

3. Place baking sheet in oven and bake until tender, about 20 minutes.

4. Remove baking sheet from oven and place carrots in a medium bowl. Toss with melted butter and enjoy immediately.

PER SERVING

Calories: 214
Fat: 11g
Protein: 1g
Sodium: 682mg

Fiber: 4g
Carbohydrates: 31g
Sugar: 24g

MASHED POTATOES

SERVES 1 | PREP: 10 MINUTES | COOK: 15 MINUTES

 This recipe calls for Yukon Gold potatoes because they have a slightly buttery flavor and are perfect for mashing. They are cooked in garlic-infused milk and cream, and mashed to perfection with tangy stone-ground mustard. Meet your new favorite!

INGREDIENTS

2 medium Yukon Gold potatoes, scrubbed and quartered

½ cup 1% milk

½ cup heavy cream

2 cloves garlic, peeled and smashed

¼ teaspoon ground coriander

1 tablespoon room temperature butter

1 tablespoon olive oil

1 tablespoon stone-ground mustard

½ teaspoon kosher salt

⅛ teaspoon freshly ground black pepper

1. Place potatoes in a 2-quart saucepan. Add milk, cream, garlic, and coriander and stir. (Add a little extra milk or cream if potatoes are not almost completely covered by the liquid.) Cook over medium-high heat 20 minutes, or until potatoes are tender and the tip of a knife can be easily inserted in the center.

2. Strain potatoes over a medium bowl and set cream mixture aside.

3. Return potatoes to pan and add ¼ cup cream mixture back into pan. Mash potatoes with a potato masher or an immersion blender.

4. Fold in butter, oil, and stone-ground mustard. Add additional leftover cream mixture to achieve the desired consistency.

5. Season with salt and pepper and enjoy.

PER SERVING

Calories: 914   Fiber: 8g
Fat: 70g   Carbohydrates: 59g
Protein: 13g   Sugar: 13g
Sodium: 1,660mg

SCALLOPED POTATOES

SERVES 1 | PREP: 10 MINUTES | COOK: 45 MINUTES

 This Scalloped Potatoes recipe is creamy, extra cheesy, and incredibly delicious! Made with just 1 medium potato, it is sure to become a favorite. The recipe uses Cheddar cheese, but feel free to substitute your favorite; Monterey jack, fontina, and Gruyère are all excellent choices.

INGREDIENTS

1 medium Yukon Gold potato, peeled, sliced, and cut into ¼" slices

1 tablespoon room temperature butter

1 tablespoon all-purpose flour

½ cup 1% milk

½ cup plus 2 tablespoons shredded Cheddar cheese, divided

⅛ teaspoon kosher salt

⅛ teaspoon freshly ground black pepper

1. Preheat oven to 375°F.

2. Spread potatoes in an even layer in a 5" × 5" baking dish (or 10-ounce ramekin) greased with butter or oil. Set aside.

3. In a 1-quart saucepan over medium heat, melt butter 30 seconds. Stir in flour and cook, stirring constantly, 2 minutes.

4. Slowly stir in milk. Cook, stirring frequently, until mixture is smooth and has thickened, about 2 minutes.

5. Stir in ½ cup cheese, salt, and pepper and continue stirring until cheese has melted, about 1 minute.

6. Pour mixture over potatoes and place dish or ramekin on a large baking sheet. Bake 25 minutes.

7. Remove from oven and top with remaining cheese. Return to oven and bake an additional 20 minutes until cheese has melted. Enjoy.

PER SERVING

Calories: 571
Fat: 36g
Protein: 24g
Sodium: 831mg

Fiber: 4g
Carbohydrates: 38g
Sugar: 8g

ROASTED BEETS WITH GOAT CHEESE

SERVES 1 | PREP: 5 MINUTES | COOK: 40 MINUTES

 Warm beets are paired with creamy, salty goat cheese and crunchy walnuts. One thing to remember about cooking with beets is that they can get messy—and that's okay! Just make sure to use a cutting board that you don't mind getting dirty. I like to use a plastic one because it's easy to wipe down. You could also line a cutting board with a few paper towels to help keep the area clean from beet juices.

INGREDIENTS

1 medium beet, top removed, peeled, and cut into 1½" chunks

1 tablespoon olive oil

½ teaspoon dried thyme

½ teaspoon kosher salt

¼ teaspoon freshly ground black pepper

¼ cup chopped walnuts

¼ cup crumbled goat cheese

1. Preheat oven to 400°F. Line a large baking sheet with aluminum foil.

2. Place cut beets on baking sheet and toss with oil, thyme, salt, and pepper.

3. Bake 35 minutes until beets are fork-tender.

4. Transfer to a large bowl, toss with walnuts and goat cheese. Enjoy warm.

PER SERVING

Calories: 475   Fiber: 5g
Fat: 43g   Carbohydrates: 13g
Protein: 14g   Sugar: 7g
Sodium: 1,379mg

CLASSIC DEVILED EGGS

SERVES 1 | PREP: 15 MINUTES | COOK: 12 MINUTES

 Deviled eggs are a classic dish to bring to parties and potlucks. But if you're craving deviled eggs and don't want to make a big batch, this recipe is for you! With a filling of yolk, mayonnaise, mustard, a touch of lemon juice, and a couple of spices, it's quick, easy, and delicious.

INGREDIENTS

2 large eggs (in shells)

1 tablespoon mayonnaise

½ tablespoon yellow mustard

¼ teaspoon lemon juice

⅛ teaspoon garlic powder

1. Gently place eggs in bottom of a 1-quart pot. Fill pot with cold water to cover eggs by at least 1".

2. Bring water to a rolling boil over high heat. Once water starts boiling, turn off heat, cover pot, and let sit on burner 12 minutes.

3. Using a slotted spoon, transfer eggs to a small bowl filled with ice water and let cool 5 minutes.

4. Once cool, peel eggs and slice them in half lengthwise. Place on a medium plate and set aside.

5. Scoop out yolks and place in a small bowl. Mash with a fork. Add mayonnaise, mustard, lemon juice, and garlic powder and mix until smooth.

6. Use a spoon to transfer filling to center of each egg. Enjoy.

Innovating Your Hard-Boiled Egg Recipe
Delicious and high in protein, eggs can be hard-boiled ahead of time and eaten over the next few days for an easy breakfast, snack, or addition to a salad. To mix things up, try topping them with hummus or guacamole, or channel your love for chicken wings by adding a drizzle of hot sauce and crumbled blue cheese.

PER SERVING

Calories: 255
Fat: 21g
Protein: 13g
Sodium: 295mg

Fiber: 0g
Carbohydrates: 2g
Sugar: 1g

SAUTÉED PEAS WITH PROSCIUTTO (PICTURED)

SERVES 1 | PREP: 5 MINUTES | COOK: 10 MINUTES

Frozen vegetables are ideal to have on hand when cooking for one; you can use the amount you need for a recipe and keep the remainder in the freezer to use later.

INGREDIENTS

½ tablespoon olive oil

2 tablespoons peeled and chopped yellow onion

1 clove garlic, peeled and minced

⅛ teaspoon kosher salt

⅛ teaspoon freshly ground black pepper

1 cup frozen peas, thawed

1 thin slice prosciutto, diced

1 tablespoon chopped fresh parsley

1. In an 8" skillet over medium heat, heat oil 30 seconds. Add onions, garlic, salt, and pepper, and sauté until tender, about 1 minute.
2. Add peas and sauté until heated through, about 3 minutes. Stir in prosciutto and cook an additional 1 minute.
3. Add parsley and remove from heat. Enjoy warm.

PER SERVING

Calories: 206 | Fat: 9g | Protein: 11g | Sodium: 671mg Fiber: 7g | Carbohydrates: 23g | Sugar: 7g

GUACAMOLE

SERVES 1 | PREP: 5 MINUTES | COOK: 0 MINUTES

Made with just one avocado combined with a touch of lime juice, onions, garlic, salt, and jalapeños, this dish is perfect served with tortilla chips, as a topping for tacos, or a spread for sandwiches.

INGREDIENTS

1 medium avocado, ripe, halved, and pitted

¼ teaspoon kosher salt

1 tablespoon lime juice

1 tablespoon peeled and chopped red onion

1 clove garlic, peeled and finely minced

⅛ teaspoon chopped jalapeños

1. Scoop out avocado flesh into a small bowl. Mash flesh with a fork, being sure to leave a few chunks.
2. Add salt, juice, onions, garlic, and jalapeños to bowl and blend gently.
3. Cover and chill in refrigerator until ready to use, or eat right away.

PER SERVING

Calories: 333 | Fat: 30g | Protein: 4g | Sodium: 597mg Fiber: 14g | Carbohydrates: 20g | Sugar: 2g

BAKED SWEET POTATO FRIES

SERVES 1 | PREP: 10 MINUTES | COOK: 20 MINUTES

 Wedges of sweet potatoes are tossed with olive oil and spices and baked until gorgeously browned. They make the perfect snack or side dish. To make them extra special, whip up a spicy mayonnaise dip by whisking together 2 tablespoons of mayonnaise and ¼ teaspoon of hot sauce. If you prefer an even spicier dipping sauce, add a drop or two more of the hot sauce.

INGREDIENTS

1 medium sweet potato, peeled and cut into ½"-thick wedges

1 tablespoon olive oil

½ teaspoon smoked paprika

¼ teaspoon garlic powder

¼ teaspoon kosher salt

⅛ teaspoon freshly ground black pepper

1. Preheat oven to 425°F.

2. Place sweet potatoes in a medium bowl and toss in oil. Sprinkle with paprika, garlic powder, salt, and pepper and mix well, so all potatoes are coated.

3. Spread potatoes in a single layer onto a large ungreased baking sheet.

4. Bake for 10 minutes, then use tongs or a fork to turn over all potato pieces and bake for another 10 minutes until browned.

5. Transfer fries to a medium plate and let cool 5 minutes before eating.

PER SERVING

Calories: 228
Fat: 14g
Protein: 3g
Sodium: 624mg

Fiber: 4g
Carbohydrates: 25g
Sugar: 8g

GARLIC SESAME GREEN BEANS

SERVES 1 | PREP: 5 MINUTES | COOK: 15 MINUTES

 These green beans are a simple, yet delicious side dish that would go perfectly with just about any entrée. They're hot and buttery, with a hint of garlic and a fresh, crisp-tender texture. The green beans are seasoned simply with just a bit of salt and pepper, but feel free to add other spices such as dried oregano, thyme, or cayenne pepper as they cook.

INGREDIENTS

1 cup fresh green beans, trimmed

¼ teaspoon kosher salt

1 tablespoon room temperature butter

1 clove garlic, peeled and minced

½ teaspoon sesame seeds

1. Place green beans in a 2-quart saucepan and cover with cold water. Add salt and bring to a boil over high heat. Once boiling, reduce heat to low and cook until beans soften, about 4 minutes.

2. Drain water from pan and set aside.

3. In a 10" skillet over medium heat, melt butter 30 seconds. Add garlic and toast until golden, 1 minute.

4. Add green beans to skillet, top with sesame seeds, and toss to coat. Enjoy immediately.

PER SERVING

Calories: 146
Fat: 12g
Protein: 2g
Sodium: 590mg

Fiber: 3g
Carbohydrates: 8g
Sugar: 3g

SWEET POTATO CASSEROLE

SERVES 1 | PREP: 5 MINUTES | COOK: 30 MINUTES

 When my family gathers for a holiday meal, one of the traditional side dishes we serve is a Sweet Potato Casserole. But why wait for a holiday? Enjoy this scaled-down recipe any time of the year! It's also the perfect dish to make if you have leftover fresh or canned sweet potatoes.

INGREDIENTS

1 cup (about 1 large) cooked, peeled, and mashed sweet potato

2 tablespoons light brown sugar

1 teaspoon ground cinnamon

½ teaspoon ground nutmeg

½ teaspoon kosher salt

¼ teaspoon allspice

¼ teaspoon ground ginger

⅛ teaspoon ground cloves

1 large egg, lightly beaten

¼ cup whole pecans

½ cup miniature marshmallows

1. Preheat oven to 350°F.

2. Place sweet potato in a large bowl.

3. In a separate smaller bowl, combine brown sugar, cinnamon, nutmeg, salt, allspice, ginger, and cloves. Stir into sweet potato.

4. Add egg to sweet potato mixture, stir, and pour into an oven-safe 2-cup ramekin (or a similar-sized baking dish) greased with butter or oil.

5. Top mixture with pecans, place on a large baking sheet, and bake 20 minutes.

6. Remove from oven and top with marshmallows. Return to the oven and bake another 10 minutes until marshmallows are melted and begin to turn golden. Enjoy.

PER SERVING

Calories: 689
Fat: 23g
Protein: 14g
Sodium: 1,351mg

Fiber: 13g
Carbohydrates: 113g
Sugar: 61g

HAM AND PINEAPPLE–STUFFED SWEET POTATO

SERVES 1 | PREP: 15 MINUTES | COOK: 50 MINUTES

 A sweet potato can make a hearty side, especially when stuffed with salty ham and sweet pineapple chunks! For convenience, sweet potatoes can be baked ahead of time and kept in the refrigerator until you're ready to use them. Try topping this Ham and Pineapple–Stuffed Sweet Potato with tangy barbecue sauce.

INGREDIENTS

1 medium sweet potato, scrubbed

½ tablespoon room temperature butter

¼ cup chopped fresh pineapple

1 tablespoon light brown sugar

⅛ teaspoon ground cinnamon

⅛ teaspoon kosher salt

¼ cup shredded Monterey jack cheese

1 slice Canadian bacon, browned

1. Preheat oven to 400°F.

2. Pierce potato several times with a fork, then rub with butter. Place on a small foil-lined baking sheet and bake 50 minutes until tender.

3. When done, allow to cool slightly, about 15 minutes, then split open with a knife. Gently press in on both ends, then scoop out potato flesh and transfer to a small bowl. (Leave skins on baking sheet.)

4. Stir in pineapple, brown sugar, cinnamon, and salt.

5. Spoon potato mixture back into skins and top with cheese and Canadian bacon. Bake until cheese has melted, about 6 minutes. Enjoy hot.

PER SERVING

Calories: 373

Fat: 15g

Protein: 15g

Sodium: 1,041mg

Fiber: 5g

Carbohydrates: 46g

Sugar: 23g

SPINACH ORZO SALAD

SERVES 1 | PREP: 10 MINUTES | COOK: 15 MINUTES

 This delightful Spinach Orzo Salad is sure to become one of your favorites. Orzo is a delicious short-cut pasta that resembles rice. Mixed with creamy feta cheese, toasted pine nuts, chopped red onions, sun-dried tomatoes, and Kalamata olives, it makes for a hearty and oh-so scrumptious lunch or dinner!

INGREDIENTS

2 ounces uncooked orzo pasta

2 cups finely chopped, loosely packed fresh spinach

¼ cup feta cheese

¼ cup peeled and chopped red onion

¼ cup toasted pine nuts

¼ cup sun-dried tomatoes, chopped

¼ cup sliced Kalamata olives

2 tablespoons olive oil

2 tablespoons balsamic vinegar

⅛ teaspoon dried basil

⅛ teaspoon freshly ground black pepper

1. Bring a small pot of water to a boil over high heat. Add orzo and cook 8 minutes or until al dente. Drain, rinse in cold water, and set aside.

2. Toss together spinach, feta cheese, onions, pine nuts, sun-dried tomatoes, and Kalamata olives in a large owl. Add cooked orzo and stir well. Set aside.

3. Whisk together oil, balsamic vinegar, basil, and pepper in a small bowl. Pour over salad and toss.

4. Cover and refrigerate at least 1 hour. Enjoy cold.

PER SERVING

Calories: 989   Fiber: 7g
Fat: 72g   Carbohydrates: 70g
Protein: 21g   Sugar: 17g
Sodium: 1,172mg

RICE PILAF

SERVES 1 | PREP: 5 MINUTES | COOK: 30 MINUTES

 Rice Pilaf is a wonderful upgrade from everyday rice and goes with just about any main protein. Toasting the rice in butter before adding the broth gives it a deep nutty aroma and a more complex flavor. I've kept this recipe simple, but you can add other ingredients such as peas or sliced mushrooms to take it to the next level.

INGREDIENTS

1 tablespoon room temperature butter

½ cup peeled, finely chopped yellow onion

1 clove garlic, peeled and minced

¼ cup long-grain white rice, rinsed

¾ cup low-sodium chicken broth

⅛ teaspoon kosher salt

1 In a 10" skillet over medium heat, melt butter 30 seconds. Add onions and garlic and cook until onions are translucent and soft, about 2 minutes.

2 Add rice and coat with butter. Continue to cook, stirring often, until rice is lightly toasted, about 4 minutes.

3 Add broth and salt and bring to a boil over high heat.

4 Once boiling, reduce to a simmer over low heat, cover, and cook 16 minutes until rice is tender.

5 Remove skillet from heat, keep covered, and let sit 5 minutes.

6 Remove lid and fluff rice with a fork. Enjoy.

Tips for Making the Best Rice Pilaf
Sauté your vegetables in butter, then add the rice and toast it for a nutty flavor. Enhance the flavor even more with your favorite broth. Also be sure to let the rice rest for at least 5 minutes after cooking before you enjoy it.

PER SERVING

Calories: 352   Fiber: 2g
Fat: 13g   Carbohydrates: 51g
Protein: 9g   Sugar: 4g
Sodium: 351mg

SAUSAGE PINE NUT DRESSING

SERVES 1 | PREP: 15 MINUTES | COOK: 30 MINUTES

 This small-batch sausage dressing is the perfect side dish to go along with turkey or chicken. It's a scaled-down version of my own family's favorite Thanksgiving dressing, but don't wait for a holiday to enjoy it yourself! Cubes of soft sourdough bread are flavored with cooked Italian sausage, fresh sage, onions, and toasted nuts to create an incredibly moist and rich dish.

INGREDIENTS

¼ cup peeled and chopped yellow onion

1 medium carrot, peeled and chopped

1 medium stalk celery, chopped

3 fresh sage leaves

½ tablespoon olive oil

6 ounces loose Italian sausage

½ teaspoon kosher salt

½ cup toasted pine nuts

2 cups cubed sourdough bread

1 large egg

½ cup low-sodium chicken broth

¼ cup heavy cream

1. Preheat oven to 375°F and grease a 5" × 5" baking dish with butter.

2. Place onions, carrots, celery, and sage in a food processor and pulse until very finely chopped.

3. Add oil to a 10" skillet over medium heat. Add sausage and cook until browned, about 5 minutes. Remove sausage from pan and place on a large paper towel–lined plate.

4. Add finely chopped vegetables to skillet and sauté until most moisture has evaporated, about 4 minutes. Remove from heat and season with salt.

5. Place vegetables, sausage, and toasted pine nuts in a large bowl. Stir in bread cubes. Set aside.

6. In a smaller bowl, whisk together egg, chicken broth, and cream. Pour over dressing mix and stir until bread is entirely moistened.

7. Pour mixture into a greased baking dish and bake until golden brown, about 30 minutes. Enjoy warm.

How to Toast Pine Nuts

Heat a small pan over medium heat for 30 seconds. Add ¼ teaspoon of oil and swirl to coat bottom of the pan. Add your pine nuts and stir frequently until they are golden brown, about 4 minutes.

PER SERVING

Calories: 1,341
Fat: 106g
Protein: 44g
Sodium: 2,351mg
Fiber: 8g
Carbohydrates: 61g
Sugar: 15g

ITALIAN PASTA SALAD

SERVES 1 | PREP: 10 MINUTES | COOK: 10 MINUTES

 A scaled-down version of a quintessential summer salad, this Italian Pasta Salad is made with chopped broccoli, salami, red peppers, feta, and mozzarella cheese and is tossed with a flavorful Italian dressing. Pair it with a burger, sandwich, grilled chicken—or whatever you like.

INGREDIENTS

½ cup rotini pasta, cooked al dente according to package instructions

⅓ cup chopped red pepper

¼ cup fresh broccoli florets

1 ounce salami, chopped

8 black olives, pitted

3 tablespoons Italian dressing

2 tablespoons crumbled feta cheese

2 tablespoons shredded mozzarella cheese

1 Combine all ingredients in a medium bowl.

2 Cover and refrigerate until cool, about 1 hour, then enjoy.

Tips for Making the Best Pasta Salad

Short pasta works best in a pasta salad. Choose a pasta shape with curves and ridges that will hold up well when tossed with your other ingredients. Cook the pasta until just slightly underdone. Overcooked pasta will fall apart when mixed with dressing. Add in the remaining ingredients when the pasta is cool.

PER SERVING

Calories: 647   Fiber: 4g
Fat: 38g   Carbohydrates: 56g
Protein: 21g   Sugar: 9g
Sodium: 2,023mg

ROASTED BUTTERNUT SQUASH SOUP

SERVES 1 | PREP: 10 MINUTES | COOK: 20 MINUTES

 This cozy Roasted Butternut Squash Soup is ready in 30 minutes! Butternut squash has a sweet, slightly nutty taste, and in this soup, the sweetness is balanced perfectly by the curry powder.

INGREDIENTS

10 ounces (about ½ large) butternut squash, peeled, seeded, and cut into ½" cubes

½ tablespoon olive oil

¼ teaspoon kosher salt

½ cup peeled and chopped yellow onion

1 clove garlic, peeled and minced

1½ cups chicken broth

1 teaspoon curry powder

½ tablespoon pure honey

1 teaspoon plain full-fat yogurt

1. Spread squash cubes on a baking sheet. Drizzle with oil and salt and bake at 425°F for 25 minutes or until the squash begins to brown and is soft to the touch.

2. In a 3.5-quart saucepan over medium heat, heat oil 30 seconds. Add onions and garlic and sauté until soft, about 6 minutes.

3. Add butternut squash, broth, and curry powder and bring to a boil over high heat. Once boiling, reduce heat to low and simmer until squash is tender, about 13 minutes.

4. Remove pan from heat and stir in honey.

5. Purée mixture in pan with an immersion blender, or pour into a stand blender and blend until smooth.

6. Pour into a medium serving bowl and add yogurt. Enjoy while hot.

What to Do with Leftover Butternut Squash

Since you will be using half of a butternut squash in this recipe, you might consider roasting the remaining squash in the oven for a wonderful side dish or salad topping.

PER SERVING

Calories: 286
Fat: 8g
Protein: 7g
Sodium: 1,908mg

Fiber: 8g
Carbohydrates: 53g
Sugar: 20g

CREAMY CARROT SOUP

SERVES 1 | PREP: 10 MINUTES | COOK: 30 MINUTES

 This Creamy Carrot Soup is made with just two carrots and gets a whole lot of flavor from the lightly browned onions and garlic. It's the perfect soup to make any time of the year. Enjoy with a piece of crusty French bread.

INGREDIENTS

1 tablespoon room temperature butter

2 large carrots, peeled and sliced

½ cup peeled and chopped yellow onion

1 clove garlic, peeled and minced

1 cup low-sodium chicken broth

¼ teaspoon kosher salt

⅛ teaspoon ground nutmeg

¼ cup heavy cream

1. In a 2-quart saucepan over medium-high heat, melt butter 30 seconds. Add carrots, onions, and garlic and cook, stirring occasionally, until vegetables are softened, about 10 minutes.

2. Add chicken broth to pan. (There should be enough to cover the vegetables. Add a little more broth if necessary.)

3. Add salt and nutmeg, and bring to a boil over high heat, then reduce heat to a simmer on medium-low and continue cooking until carrots are cooked through, about 10 minutes.

4. Purée the soup in the pot using an immersion blender, or pour into a stand blender and blend until smooth.

5. Pour into a medium bowl, stir in cream, and enjoy while hot.

PER SERVING

Calories: 441

Fat: 35g

Protein: 9g

Sodium: 774mg

Fiber: 6g

Carbohydrates: 27g

Sugar: 12g

FRENCH ONION SOUP

SERVES 1 | PREP: 10 MINUTES | COOK: 50 MINUTES

 A bowl of French Onion Soup is a perfect side for a sandwich, but also makes a great lunch or dinner when you aren't as hungry. Made with one onion and a handful of other simple ingredients, this comforting soup can be on your table in about an hour. While this recipe uses a small onion, a slightly larger one just means a soup with more wonderful onions: not a bad problem to have!

INGREDIENTS

3 tablespoons room temperature butter

1 small yellow onion, peeled, halved lengthwise, and thinly sliced

1 clove garlic, peeled and chopped

½ teaspoon dried thyme

¼ teaspoon kosher salt

⅛ teaspoon freshly ground black pepper

¼ cup dry red wine

1 tablespoon all-purpose flour

2 cups chicken broth

1 thick slice French bread

¼ cup shredded Gruyère cheese

1. In a 2-quart saucepan over medium heat, melt butter 30 seconds. Add onions, garlic, thyme, salt, and pepper and cook until onions are very soft and caramelized, about 25 minutes.

2. Add wine, bring to a boil over high heat, then reduce heat to medium-low and simmer until the wine has evaporated, about 5 minutes.

3. Sprinkle flour over onions and stir, then continue cooking for 10 minutes, stirring occasionally so flour doesn't burn.

4. Stir in broth and bring soup back to a simmer over medium heat, and cook for 10 more minutes.

5. Heat broiler to low. Place French bread onto a small ungreased baking sheet. Sprinkle cheese over top and broil until cheese is bubbly and golden brown, about 3 minutes.

6. Place bread in a medium soup bowl and pour soup over top. Enjoy immediately.

What to Do with Leftover Wine

You can freeze wine by pouring it into ice cube trays and placing the trays in the freezer. When you want to use a little wine in a recipe, pop out one of the frozen wine cubes and add it to your recipe!

PER SERVING

Calories: 901 *Fiber: 5g*
Fat: 48g *Carbohydrates: 89g*
Protein: 28g *Sugar: 12g*
Sodium: 3,365mg

PEAR SALAD WITH BLUE CHEESE CRUMBLES

SERVES 1 | PREP: 5 MINUTES | COOK: 0 MINUTES

 This fresh, healthy salad is a delightful alternative to the typical green salad and will make a great addition to your dinner table. A simple yet flavorful orange vinaigrette drizzled over the top takes things to a whole new level. You can also substitute the blue cheese for feta if you prefer.

INGREDIENTS

½ small pear, cored and thinly sliced

¼ cup peeled and sliced red onion

1 cup loosely packed spring mix

¼ cup smoked almonds, chopped

2 tablespoons blue cheese crumbles

1 tablespoon pulp-free orange juice

1 tablespoon olive oil

½ tablespoon apple cider vinegar

¼ teaspoon granulated sugar

⅛ teaspoon kosher salt

⅛ teaspoon freshly ground black pepper

1. In a large bowl, gently toss together pear, onion, lettuce, almonds, and blue cheese. Set aside.

2. In a separate small bowl, whisk together orange juice, oil, vinegar, sugar, salt, and pepper.

3. Pour dressing over salad and gently toss to coat. Enjoy immediately.

PER SERVING

Calories: 395
Fat: 30g
Protein: 11g
Sodium: 551mg

Fiber: 7g
Carbohydrates: 25g
Sugar: 13g

KALE SALAD WITH APPLES (PICTURED)

SERVES 1 | PREP: 10 MINUTES | COOK: 0 MINUTES

For a twist, substitute walnuts or pecans for the almonds, and cranberries or another dried fruit favorite for the blueberries.

INGREDIENTS

½ tablespoon apple cider vinegar

1 tablespoon olive oil

1 teaspoon pure honey

½ teaspoon lemon juice

⅛ teaspoon kosher salt

2 cups fresh kale

1 small red apple, peeled, cored, and diced

2 tablespoons dried blueberries

1 tablespoon slivered almonds

1. In a small bowl, whisk together vinegar, oil, honey, lemon juice, and salt. Set aside.

2. Place kale in a medium bowl. Toss in apples, blueberries, and almonds.

3. Pour vinaigrette over salad and toss. Enjoy immediately.

PER SERVING

Calories: 317 | Fat: 17g | Protein: 3g | Sodium: 306mg
Fiber: 7g | Carbohydrates: 43g | Sugar: 32g

WALDORF SALAD

SERVES 1 | PREP: 10 MINUTES | COOK: 0 MINUTES

The popular Waldorf Salad was first introduced at the Waldorf Astoria Hotel in 1893. To make a heartier version, try adding ¼ cup cooked, chopped chicken or turkey to the recipe.

INGREDIENTS

2 tablespoons mayonnaise

1 teaspoon lemon juice

⅛ teaspoon kosher salt

1 small red apple, cored and chopped

¼ cup thinly sliced celery

½ cup fresh green grapes, sliced in half

2 tablespoons chopped walnuts

4 large leaves romaine lettuce

1. In a medium bowl, whisk together mayonnaise, lemon juice, and salt. Stir in apple, celery, grapes, and walnuts.

2. Spoon salad over lettuce on a medium plate and enjoy.

PER SERVING

Calories: 425 | Fat: 31g | Protein: 4g | Sodium: 493mg
Fiber: 6g | Carbohydrates: 39g | Sugar: 29g

CHAPTER FOUR
CHICKEN MAIN DISHES

Chicken is my top "go-to" meat. From grilling it in the backyard, to searing it on the stove, to baking it in the oven, cooking chicken is simple, and the recipes are endless. Chicken is also one of the least expensive meats you can buy, both fresh and frozen. This light meat provides a wonderful base that you can enhance with any herbs, spices, and other ingredients you already have on hand. Plus it cooks relatively quickly, meaning that in a short period of time you can be enjoying a great meal.

The single-serving chicken recipes in this chapter are easy, quick, and intensely satisfying. Be sure to try the Cashew Chicken when you're craving takeout. And if you're at home watching a sporting event on TV, the Baked Chicken Tenders are a must-try. You'll also find my tried-and-true recipe for Chicken Enchiladas—my daughter's favorite meal growing up. You'll want to soak up every last bite. Enjoy!

BUTTER CHICKEN

SERVES 1 | PREP: 30 MINUTES | COOK: 30 MINUTES

 This is the easiest chicken recipe you'll ever find! It features tender cubes of chicken cooked in a mildly spiced curry. Once you see just how quickly it all comes together, you might find yourself skipping takeout. Pair with a salad or Honey-Roasted Carrots (see recipe in Chapter 3).

INGREDIENTS

For Marinade

½ cup sour cream

½ tablespoon lemon juice

½ tablespoon ground turmeric

½ tablespoon garam masala

½ tablespoon ground cumin

1 (6-ounce) boneless, skinless chicken breast, cut into 1" pieces

For Chicken

2 tablespoons room temperature butter, divided

½ cup peeled and chopped yellow onion

1 clove garlic, peeled and minced

½ teaspoon ground cumin

¼ teaspoon ground ginger

¼ teaspoon ground cinnamon

¼ teaspoon kosher salt

1 cup tomato sauce

¼ cup heavy cream

1 cup cooked white rice

1. **To make Marinade:** Mix together sour cream, lemon juice, turmeric, garam masala, and cumin in a medium bowl. Add chicken pieces and stir so that all pieces are completely covered. Cover bowl and refrigerate for at least 30 minutes.

1. **To make Chicken:** Melt 1 tablespoon butter in a 10" skillet over medium-high heat for 30 seconds. Add onions and cook 3 minutes, stirring occasionally. Add garlic, cumin, ginger, cinnamon, and salt and cook an additional 2 minutes.

2. Stir in tomato sauce and reduce heat to low.

3. While sauce is simmering on low, melt remaining tablespoon butter in a separate 8" skillet over medium-high heat for 30 seconds.

4. Add chicken to second skillet and cook 5 minutes on each side until browned.

5. Remove chicken from skillet and add to sauce. Simmer another 10 minutes.

6. Stir in cream and cook, stirring occasionally, another 1 minute. Serve over rice and enjoy.

PER SERVING

Calories: 944
Fat: 53g
Protein: 49g
Sodium: 1,848mg

Fiber: 7g
Carbohydrates: 70g
Sugar: 14g

CHICKEN ALFREDO

SERVES 1 | PREP: 5 MINUTES | COOK: 15 MINUTES

 Tender, golden chicken is cooked in butter and garlic and simmered in a rich and creamy homemade Alfredo sauce. Ideal for spooning over pasta. For a low-carb meal, enjoy with spaghetti squash. Alfredo sauce is so easy to make that once you make your own, you'll never go back to jarred sauce again.

INGREDIENTS

1 (6-ounce) boneless, skinless chicken breast

¼ teaspoon kosher salt, divided

⅛ teaspoon freshly ground black pepper

1 tablespoon room temperature butter, divided

1 clove garlic, peeled and minced

½ cup heavy cream

½ teaspoon lemon juice

⅛ teaspoon ground nutmeg

2 tablespoons grated Parmesan cheese

1 cup cooked fettuccini pasta

1 Season chicken breast with ⅛ teaspoon salt and pepper. Set aside.

2 In a 10" skillet over medium-high heat, melt ½ tablespoon butter 30 seconds. Add chicken and cook 4 minutes on each side until golden brown.

3 Transfer chicken to a medium plate, cover, and set aside.

4 Add remaining ½ tablespoon butter to same pan and melt 30 seconds, then add garlic and cook, stirring constantly, 1 minute.

5 Pour cream into pan and whisk in lemon juice, nutmeg, and remaining salt. Cook, stirring constantly, 2 minutes until thickened.

6 Add Parmesan cheese and stir 1 minute.

7 Slice chicken into ½" thick slices and add to sauce. Stir 1 minute.

8 Pour chicken and sauce over pasta on a medium plate and enjoy.

PER SERVING

Calories: 1,000   Fiber: 3g
Fat: 64g   Carbohydrates: 51g
Protein: 55g   Sugar: 4g
Sodium: 1,060mg

LEMON AND GARLIC CHICKEN

SERVES 1 | PREP: 20 MINUTES | COOK: 25 MINUTES

 Easy to make and full of flavor, this Lemon and Garlic Chicken is one for your recipe file. This wonderful recipe begins with a flavorful marinade that gives the chicken so much flavor. For a low-carb variation, enjoy in a lettuce wrap.

INGREDIENTS

For Marinade

1 clove garlic, peeled and minced

2 tablespoons lemon juice

1 tablespoon olive oil

½ teaspoon smoked paprika

½ teaspoon Italian seasoning

¼ teaspoon kosher salt

¼ teaspoon freshly ground black pepper

For Chicken

1 (6-ounce) boneless, skinless chicken breast

½ cup uncooked orzo (approximately 4 ounces)

½ tablespoon butter

1. **To make Marinade:** Combine garlic, lemon juice, oil, paprika, Italian seasoning, salt, and pepper in a small bowl.

1. **To make Chicken:** Place chicken breast in a medium shallow dish and pour marinade over top. Cover dish and refrigerate for at least 20 minutes.

2. Preheat oven to 350°F.

3. Remove chicken from refrigerator and place onto a small ungreased baking sheet. Bake 25 minutes until completely cooked through.

4. Remove chicken from oven, cover with a piece of foil, and let rest 10 minutes.

5. While the chicken is resting, make orzo by filling a 2-quart pot three-quarters full with lightly salted water and bringing to a boil over high heat. Add orzo to pot and boil 8 minutes, or until it has a firm, chewy texture. (Stir occasionally while cooking to prevent orzo from sticking together.)

6. Drain orzo and add back into warm pot. Stir in butter.

7. Slice chicken and enjoy over cooked orzo on a medium plate.

PER SERVING

Calories: 804   Fiber: 4g
Fat: 26g   Carbohydrates: 89g
Protein: 54g   Sugar: 6g
Sodium: 666mg

CASHEW CHICKEN

SERVES 1 | PREP: 5 MINUTES | COOK: 15 MINUTES

Cashew Chicken for one: easy to make and so much better than takeout! Tender cooked chicken and cashews are served with a sweet garlic sauce. The recipe calls for using ground ginger for convenience, but you can use ¼ teaspoon of freshly grated ginger instead if preferred. This single-serving version of Cashew Chicken is full of flavor, healthy, and can be ready in minutes!

INGREDIENTS

For Sauce

2 tablespoons low-sodium soy sauce

2 tablespoons pure honey

1 teaspoon olive oil

⅛ teaspoon ground ginger

1 tablespoon water

For Chicken

1 (6-ounce) boneless, skinless chicken breast, cut into 1" cubes

⅛ teaspoon kosher salt

⅛ teaspoon freshly ground black pepper

½ tablespoon olive oil

½ cup peeled and thickly chopped yellow onion

½ cup fresh broccoli florets

1 clove garlic, peeled and minced

¼ cup unsalted cashews

1 cup cooked white rice

PER SERVING

Calories: 899   Fiber: 4g
Fat: 32g   Carbohydrates: 103g
Protein: 53g   Sugar: 40g
Sodium: 1,541mg

1. **To make Sauce:** Whisk together soy sauce, honey, oil, ginger, and water in a small bowl. Set aside.

1. **To make Chicken:** Season chicken with salt and pepper. Heat oil in a 10" skillet over medium-high heat 30 seconds. Add chicken and sauté until cooked through, about 4 minutes.

2. Add onions, broccoli, and garlic to skillet. Cook, stirring occasionally, one minute until vegetables are crisp-tender.

3. Add cashews and sauce. Cook until mixture comes to a light boil, then reduce heat to low and simmer 3 minutes.

4. Enjoy on a medium plate with cooked rice.

Cooking Rice for One Tip

Cook a large batch of brown or white rice and freeze it in individual portions using a muffin pan. Once frozen, pop the rice discs out of the muffin pan and freeze in a zip-top bag. Whenever you need a single serving of rice, just heat up one of the frozen discs.

WHITE CHICKEN CHILI

SERVES 1 | PREP: 5 MINUTES | COOK: 20 MINUTES

 A twist on traditional beef chili, this White Chicken Chili is hearty and satisfying. It's the perfect recipe to use up rotisserie chicken or other leftover chicken. If you can't find cannellini beans, Great Northern beans make a great substitute. Also feel free to use jarred jalapeños instead of fresh, and enjoy with sour cream, shredded Monterey jack cheese, chopped cilantro, and tortilla chips, if desired.

INGREDIENTS

1 tablespoon olive oil, divided

1 (6-ounce) boneless, skinless chicken breast, cut into 1" strips

¼ teaspoon kosher salt, divided

⅛ teaspoon freshly ground black pepper

½ cup peeled and chopped yellow onion

1 clove garlic, peeled and minced

1 tablespoon finely chopped jalapeños

1 cup low-sodium chicken broth

½ cup canned cannellini beans, drained and rinsed

½ teaspoon dried oregano

¼ teaspoon ground cumin

1. In a 10" skillet over medium-high heat, heat ½ tablespoon oil 30 seconds. Place chicken in pan and season with ⅛ teaspoon salt and pepper. Cook each side 5 minutes.

2. Remove chicken from skillet and place on a medium plate. Cover plate and set aside.

3. Add ½ tablespoon oil to skillet and swirl skillet to evenly coat. Stir in onions, garlic, and jalapeños. Cook, stirring occasionally, until onions are translucent, about 3 minutes.

4. Stir in chicken broth, beans, oregano, cumin, and remaining salt. Bring to a boil over high heat.

5. Once boiling, reduce heat to a simmer over low heat and cook, stirring occasionally, 15 minutes.

6. Add chicken to pan and simmer an additional 5 minutes, then pour chili into a medium bowl and enjoy hot.

What to Do with Leftover Beans
Since you'll be using a half can of beans in this recipe, consider freezing the remainder in a freezer-safe container until ready to use. If you plan on using the beans within the next few days, you can keep them in an airtight container in the refrigerator. Use leftover beans in soups, stews, burritos, or even scrambled eggs for breakfast.

PER SERVING

Calories: 499   Fiber: 7g
Fat: 20g   Carbohydrates: 29g
Protein: 51g   Sugar: 4g
Sodium: 899mg

SWEET AND SPICY BAKED CHICKEN WINGS

SERVES 1 | PREP: 25 MINUTES | COOK: 45 MINUTES

 These tender and juicy baked chicken wings are coated with a sweet and spicy sauce that will catch your taste buds by surprise! Baked, not fried, and full of flavor, these wings are super easy to make. Enjoy with your favorite dipping sauces.

INGREDIENTS

2 tablespoons barbecue sauce

1 tablespoon pulp-free orange juice

1 teaspoon pure honey

1 teaspoon Dijon mustard

⅛ teaspoon hot sauce

1 pound skinless chicken wings

1. Mix barbecue sauce, orange juice, honey, mustard, and hot sauce together in a large bowl. Add chicken wings and toss to coat. Cover and refrigerate at least 20 minutes.

2. Preheat oven to 425°F.

3. Place wings in a single layer on a small ungreased baking pan. Bake 40 minutes until brown and crispy. Enjoy while warm.

PER SERVING

Calories: 400   Fiber: 0g

Fat: 9g   Carbohydrates: 21g

Protein: 54g   Sugar: 18g

Sodium: 672mg

SOUTHWESTERN CHICKEN WRAP

SERVES 1 | PREP: 10 MINUTES | COOK: 0 MINUTES

 This tasty chicken wrap comes together quickly with either cooked chicken left over from a previous meal, or rotisserie chicken from your grocer. If you want to cook the chicken up fresh while making the recipe, simply cook a boneless, skinless chicken breast or thigh in a small skillet with ½ tablespoon of oil for about 6 minutes, until the chicken is completely cooked through.

INGREDIENTS

1 tablespoon mild salsa

1 tablespoon ranch dressing

⅛ teaspoon ground cumin

¼ cup cooked, skinless, boneless, shredded chicken

1 Bibb lettuce leaf

1 (8") flour tortilla

2 tablespoons canned black beans, not including juice

4 fresh cherry tomatoes, sliced in half

2 tablespoons shredded Monterey jack cheese

1. Combine salsa, ranch dressing, cumin, and chicken in a small bowl.

2. Place lettuce leaf in center of tortilla. Spoon chicken mixture over lettuce and top with remaining ingredients.

3. Roll up tortilla and enjoy.

PER SERVING

Calories: 384
Fat: 16g
Protein: 22g
Sodium: 646mg

Fiber: 4g
Carbohydrates: 38g
Sugar: 4g

CHICKEN WITH CREAMY PAPRIKA SAUCE

SERVES 1 | PREP: 5 MINUTES | COOK: 20 MINUTES

 Rich and smoky, this Chicken with Creamy Paprika Sauce is wonderful served over pasta or rice. Although paprika is made from peppers that have been dried and smoked, it is not a hot spice—it is actually quite mild. When using smoked paprika, it's important to remember that a little will go a long way; when paprika is heated, the flavors come alive. Expect a warm, smoky, more complex flavor.

INGREDIENTS

1 (6-ounce) boneless, skinless chicken breast, cut into ½" strips

2 teaspoons smoked paprika, divided

⅛ teaspoon kosher salt

⅛ teaspoon freshly ground black pepper

1 tablespoon cold butter, divided

¼ cup peeled and chopped yellow onion

1 clove garlic, peeled and minced

½ cup canned diced tomatoes, including juice

½ cup low-sodium chicken broth

2 tablespoons heavy cream

1. Sprinkle all sides of chicken pieces with ½ teaspoon smoked paprika, salt, and pepper. Set aside.
2. In a 10" skillet over medium-high heat, melt ½ tablespoon butter 30 seconds.
3. Add chicken to skillet and cook 4 minutes on each side until cooked through. Transfer chicken to a large plate, cover, and set aside.
4. Melt remaining ½ tablespoon butter in skillet 30 seconds. Add chopped onions and garlic and cook, stirring occasionally, 2 minutes.
5. Add remaining smoked paprika and stir 10 seconds. Pour in diced tomatoes and cook, stirring occasionally, 1 minute.
6. Add broth and bring to a boil over high heat. Once boiling, reduce heat to medium-low and cook, stirring occasionally, 5 minutes until sauce thickens.
7. Add chicken pieces back to pan, reduce heat to low, and add cream. Stir until heated through.
8. Transfer back to medium plate and enjoy.

PER SERVING

Calories: 500   Fiber: 5g
Fat: 29g   Carbohydrates: 18g
Protein: 45g   Sugar: 9g
Sodium: 643mg

What to Do with Leftover Canned Tomatoes

Transform leftover canned tomatoes into a quick salsa! Just add chopped onions, chopped green peppers, a touch of salt, lime juice, and black pepper.

CHICKEN SOFT TACOS WITH CORN SALSA

SERVES 1 | PREP: 10 MINUTES | COOK: 15 MINUTES

 These delicious Chicken Soft Tacos with Corn Salsa make the perfect meal when you want dinner on the table quickly. One chicken breast is cooked in a skillet, piled high over warm flour tortillas, and topped with a delightful corn salsa. For optional toppings consider sour cream, shredded cheese, chopped cilantro, and a squeeze of a fresh lime.

INGREDIENTS

1 tablespoon cold butter

1 (6-ounce) boneless, skinless chicken breast, cut into ½" strips

¼ teaspoon kosher salt, divided

¼ teaspoon freshly ground black pepper, divided

2 (8") flour tortillas

½ cup frozen corn, thawed

1 small Roma tomato, chopped

1 tablespoon peeled finely chopped yellow onion

1 teaspoon chopped jalapeños

1. Preheat oven to 350°F.

2. In a 10" skillet over medium-high heat, melt butter 30 seconds.

3. Sprinkle all sides of chicken pieces with ⅛ teaspoon salt and ⅛ teaspoon pepper. Place seasoned chicken in skillet and cook 6 minutes until all pieces are cooked through. Transfer to a medium plate, cover, and set aside.

4. Wrap tortillas in foil and place on an ungreased baking sheet. Bake 5 minutes.

5. While tortillas are baking, make salsa: Combine corn, tomatoes, onions, and jalapeños in a small bowl. Season with remaining salt and pepper. Set aside.

6. To assemble tacos, fill warmed tortillas with cooked chicken, then top with corn salsa. Enjoy.

PER SERVING

Calories: 701
Fat: 24g
Protein: 50g
Sodium: 1,134mg

Fiber: 6g
Carbohydrates: 72g
Sugar: 4g

BAKED CHICKEN PARMESAN

SERVES 1 | PREP: 10 MINUTES | COOK: 30 MINUTES

 Using just a small baking dish and a few simple ingredients, this delicious Chicken Parmesan is easy to make and perfect for any night of the week. To round out the meal, enjoy with buttered pasta or white rice.

INGREDIENTS

1 tablespoon butter, melted, plus ½ tablespoon butter, divided

3 tablespoons seasoned bread crumbs

1 tablespoon grated Parmesan cheese

1 (6-ounce) boneless, skinless chicken breast

¼ cup marinara sauce

3 tablespoons shredded mozzarella cheese

1 Preheat oven to 450°F. Lightly spray a small baking dish with cooking spray.

2 Place melted butter in a medium bowl. Set aside.

3 Combine bread crumbs and Parmesan cheese in a separate small bowl.

4 Dip chicken breast in melted butter, then dredge in bread crumb mixture to coat. Place on baking sheet and top with remaining ½ tablespoon butter.

5 Bake chicken 25 minutes.

6 Remove from oven, spoon marinara sauce over chicken, and top with shredded mozzarella cheese. Bake an additional 5 minutes until cheese is melted.

7 Transfer to a medium plate and enjoy immediately.

For the Juiciest Chicken
After removing chicken from the oven, cover it with a sheet of aluminum foil for at least 5 minutes, up to 10 minutes before serving so that the juices will soak back into the meat rather than pouring out as you cut it.

PER SERVING

Calories: 560
Fat: 30g
Protein: 49g
Sodium: 884mg

Fiber: 2g
Carbohydrates: 21g
Sugar: 5g

CHICKEN WITH HERB-ROASTED TOMATOES AND GARLIC

SERVES 1 | PREP: 5 MINUTES | COOK: 30 MINUTES

 This chicken dinner is bursting with flavor! One chicken breast is surrounded by sweet cherry tomatoes and seasoned simply with oil, salt, and herbes de Provence (a delicious mix of dried spices that include rosemary, thyme, and lavender).

INGREDIENTS

1 (6-ounce) boneless, skinless chicken breast

9 fresh cherry tomatoes

1 tablespoon olive oil

⅛ teaspoon kosher salt

¼ teaspoon herbes de Provence

1. Preheat oven to 425°F.
2. Place chicken in a 9.5" baking dish lightly greased with cooking spray. Scatter tomatoes around chicken.
3. Top chicken and tomatoes with oil and season with salt and herbes de Provence.
4. Place pan in oven and bake 30 minutes.
5. Transfer to a medium plate and enjoy immediately.

PER SERVING

Calories: 352
Fat: 18g
Protein: 40g
Sodium: 375mg

Fiber: 2g
Carbohydrates: 6g
Sugar: 4g

CHICKEN PESTO PASTA

SERVES 1 | PREP: 10 MINUTES | COOK: 20 MINUTES

 This Chicken Pesto Pasta is one of those dishes that takes minutes to make, yet tastes like you've spent hours in the kitchen. You'll love it because it can be made with several kitchen shortcuts: Use jarred pasta instead of making your own, and consider rotisserie chicken or already-cooked chicken left over from a previous meal.

INGREDIENTS

½ teaspoon olive oil

1 (6-ounce) boneless, skinless chicken breast, cut into ½" strips

⅛ teaspoon kosher salt

⅛ teaspoon freshly ground black pepper

¼ cup pesto

1 tablespoon heavy cream

½ cup (about 2 ounces) rotini pasta, cooked according to package instructions

1 teaspoon grated Parmesan cheese

1. In a 10" skillet over medium heat, heat oil 30 seconds. Place chicken in skillet, season with salt and pepper, and cook 6 minutes until all pieces are cooked through. Transfer chicken to a large plate, cover, and set aside.

2. Reduce heat to low and add pesto and cream to skillet. Stir well. Add cooked pasta and chicken and toss to combine.

3. Top with Parmesan cheese, then transfer to a medium plate and enjoy while warm.

PER SERVING

Calories: 760

Fat: 40g

Protein: 50g

Sodium: 1,190mg

Fiber: 4g

Carbohydrates: 47g

Sugar: 2g

SPICY CHICKEN SANDWICH

SERVES 1 | PREP: 15 MINUTES | COOK: 10 MINUTES

 This delicious sandwich features cooked chicken topped with cheese, crispy bacon, lettuce, tomatoes, and sliced avocados. It is made extra special through the use of a popular "secret sauce" (mayonnaise with a few drops of hot sauce). Feel free to add more hot sauce if you like your sandwiches a little on the spicier side.

INGREDIENTS

1 (6-ounce) boneless, skinless chicken breast, cut into ½" pieces

⅛ teaspoon kosher salt

⅛ teaspoon freshly ground black pepper

½ tablespoon butter

1 tablespoon mayonnaise

2 drops hot sauce

1 white bulkie roll

1 Bibb lettuce leaf

1 slice vine-ripe tomato

2 slices cooked bacon

1 slice Monterey jack cheese

½ small avocado, pitted, peeled, and sliced

1. Season chicken with salt and pepper.

2. In a 10" skillet over medium-high heat, melt butter 30 seconds. Add chicken and cook 6 minutes until all pieces are cooked through. Transfer to a medium plate, cover, and set aside.

3. In a small bowl, mix together mayonnaise and hot sauce. Spread over both halves of sandwich roll.

4. Place lettuce on bottom half of sandwich roll. Top with tomato, bacon, chicken, cheese, and avocado slices, then top with sandwich roll top. Enjoy.

PER SERVING

Calories: 600
Fat: 25g
Protein: 47g
Sodium: 947mg

Fiber: 7g
Carbohydrates: 48g
Sugar: 8g

CHICKEN AND PEPPERS SHEET PAN DINNER

SERVES 1 | PREP: 10 MINUTES | COOK: 30 MINUTES

 Sheet pan meals are what dinner dreams are made of; everything bakes on one pan for easy cleanup! This Chicken and Peppers Sheet Pan Dinner definitely deserves a spot on your regular meal plan: It's low in carbs and calories, and cooks in just 30 minutes.

INGREDIENTS

1 (6-ounce) boneless, skinless chicken breast

2 teaspoons olive oil, divided

¼ teaspoon Italian seasoning, divided

¼ teaspoon kosher salt, divided

¼ teaspoon freshly ground black pepper, divided

1 small red pepper, sliced and seeded

¼ small yellow onion, peeled and sliced

2 tablespoons grated Parmesan cheese

1. Preheat oven to 400°F.

2. Rub chicken breast with ½ teaspoon oil and season with ⅛ teaspoon Italian seasoning, ⅛ teaspoon salt, and ⅛ teaspoon pepper. Place on a small, ungreased rimmed baking sheet. Set aside.

3. Combine peppers and onions in a small bowl. Add remaining oil, Italian seasoning, salt, and pepper and toss to coat.

4. Spread vegetables in a single layer on baking sheet around chicken.

5. Place sheet in oven and bake 30 minutes until chicken is cooked through.

6. Remove pan from oven and sprinkle Parmesan cheese over chicken and vegetables, then spoon onto a medium plate and enjoy hot.

PER SERVING

Calories: 361
Fat: 16g
Protein: 43g
Sodium: 832mg

Fiber: 2g
Carbohydrates: 8g
Sugar: 4g

BAKED CHICKEN CAPRESE

SERVES 1 | PREP: 5 MINUTES | COOK: 35 MINUTES

 Healthy Baked Chicken Caprese: an easy recipe filled with flavor! An Italian dish, Caprese is made with tomato, balsamic, and mozzarella cheese, and can be enjoyed as a simple salad, or over chicken.

INGREDIENTS

1 (6-ounce) boneless skinless chicken breast

½ tablespoon olive oil

¼ teaspoon dried basil

¼ teaspoon dried oregano

⅛ teaspoon garlic powder

⅛ teaspoon kosher salt

⅛ teaspoon freshly ground black pepper

1 large Roma tomato, quartered

⅓ cup peeled and chopped red onion

1 tablespoon balsamic vinegar

½ cup shredded mozzarella cheese

1. Preheat oven to 425°F.

2. Place chicken breast in a 9.5" baking dish lightly greased with cooking spray. Sprinkle with oil, basil, oregano, garlic powder, salt, and pepper.

3. Place tomatoes and onions around chicken. Drizzle balsamic over tops of chicken and vegetables.

4. Place dish in oven and bake 30 minutes.

5. Remove from oven, sprinkle mozzarella cheese over top, and bake an additional 5 minutes until cheese has melted.

6. Transfer to a medium plate and enjoy.

Chicken Tips
Consider keeping chicken pieces in the freezer so you can easily pull one out, defrost it, and cook it when ready. Look for chicken breasts (or thighs) and purchase them when they're on sale. Then, immediately divide, individually wrap, and freeze pieces for later use. The USDA recommends freezing chicken breasts no longer than nine months for optimal quality.

PER SERVING

Calories: 503   Fiber: 3g
Fat: 24g   Carbohydrates: 17g
Protein: 53g   Sugar: 10g
Sodium: 734mg

CHICKEN WITH MUSTARD TARRAGON SAUCE

SERVES 1 | PREP: 5 MINUTES | COOK: 20 MINUTES

A single-serving version of a classic French dish! One chicken breast is cooked in a velvety smooth and creamy mustard tarragon sauce. Enjoy over rice or pasta.

INGREDIENTS

½ tablespoon cold butter

1 (6-ounce) boneless, skinless chicken breast, sliced into ½" strips

¼ teaspoon kosher salt

⅛ teaspoon freshly ground black pepper

¼ cup heavy cream

1 teaspoon Dijon mustard

½ teaspoon dried tarragon

1. In a 10" skillet over medium heat, melt butter 30 seconds.

2. Sprinkle chicken with salt and pepper and add to skillet. Brown chicken on all sides, about 6 minutes total, until completely cooked through.

3. Transfer chicken to a large plate, cover, and set aside.

4. Add cream to skillet, scraping up brown bits from sides of skillet.

5. Stir in mustard and tarragon. Cook over medium-low heat, stirring constantly, until sauce thickens slightly, about 5 minutes.

6. Add chicken back to skillet and stir to coat each piece with sauce.

7. Transfer to a medium plate and serve.

PER SERVING

Calories: 466

Fat: 32g

Protein: 40g

Sodium: 795mg

Fiber: 0g

Carbohydrates: 2g

Sugar: 2g

CHICKEN ENCHILADAS

SERVES 1 | PREP: 10 MINUTES | COOK: 30 MINUTES

These small-batch enchiladas are cheesy and creamy. Each tortilla is stuffed with thick pieces of chicken and Monterey jack cheese. Top them with additional shredded cheese, chopped tomatoes, and chopped jalapeños, if desired. This recipe is especially great for when you have leftover chicken from a previous meal.

INGREDIENTS

1 tablespoon cold butter, divided

1 (6-ounce) boneless, skinless chicken breast, chopped into 1" pieces

4 tablespoons peeled and chopped yellow onion

1 clove garlic, peeled and minced

¼ teaspoon kosher salt, divided

¼ teaspoon ground coriander

⅛ teaspoon ground cumin

⅛ teaspoon freshly ground black pepper

1 tablespoon all-purpose flour

¼ cup sour cream

¾ cup chicken broth

¾ cup shredded Monterey jack cheese, divided

2 (8") flour tortillas

1. In an 8" skillet over medium-high heat, melt ½ tablespoon butter 30 seconds.

2. Place chicken in skillet and cook 6 minutes until all pieces are cooked through. Transfer chicken to a large plate, cover, and set aside.

3. In a 1-quart saucepan, melt remaining ½ tablespoon butter over medium-high heat 30 seconds. Add onions, garlic, ⅛ teaspoon of salt, coriander, cumin, and pepper. Cook, stirring occasionally, until onions are tender, about 5 minutes.

4. In a small bowl, stir flour into sour cream, then add to onion mixture in saucepan.

5. Stir in broth and remaining salt, then cook, stirring constantly, until sauce is thickened and bubbly, about 5 minutes.

6. Remove pan from heat and stir in all but 4 tablespoons cheese plus cooked chicken.

7. Divide chicken mixture between two tortillas. Add 1 tablespoon more shredded cheese to each tortilla and roll up. Arrange rolls, seam-side down, on a 5" × 5" baking dish greased with butter or oil.

8. Top dish with remaining sauce and cheese, cover with aluminum foil, then bake 30 minutes until heated through and cheese is melted.

9. Remove from oven and let stand 10 minutes before serving.

PER SERVING

Calories: 1,100 Fiber: 5g
Fat: 59g Carbohydrates: 69g
Protein: 72g Sugar: 5g
Sodium: 2,310mg

CHICKEN COBB SALAD

SERVES 1 | PREP: 10 MINUTES | COOK: 0 MINUTES

 The Cobb Salad was created by Robert Cobb, owner of the famous Brown Derby restaurant, in Los Angeles in 1937. It consists of chopped lettuce greens topped with bacon, tomatoes, avocados, blue cheese, chicken, hard-boiled eggs, and a zippy red wine vinaigrette. It's a hearty main dish salad perfect for lunch or dinner. Feel free to use your favorite bottled Italian dressing instead of making your own.

INGREDIENTS

For Salad

2 cups romaine lettuce, cut into small pieces

2 tablespoons blue cheese crumbles

2 slices cooked bacon, crumbled

1 hard-boiled egg, peeled and chopped

1 small vine-ripe tomato, chopped

1 cup cooked chopped chicken

½ medium avocado, peeled, pitted, and chopped

For Vinaigrette

1 teaspoon olive oil

1 teaspoon red wine vinegar

½ teaspoon lemon juice

⅛ teaspoon Worcestershire sauce

⅛ teaspoon garlic powder

1. **To make Salad:** Arrange lettuce on a medium plate. Top with blue cheese, bacon, egg, tomato, chicken, and avocado.

1. **To make Vinaigrette:** In a small bowl, whisk together oil, vinegar, lemon juice, Worcestershire sauce, and garlic powder. Drizzle over salad and enjoy immediately.

PER SERVING

Calories: 683   Fiber: 10g
Fat: 42g   Carbohydrates: 17g
Protein: 62g   Sugar: 5g
Sodium: 1,241mg

GREEK CHICKEN AND PASTA

SERVES 1 | PREP: 10 MINUTES | COOK: 20 MINUTES

 The healthy, flavorful ingredients of the Mediterranean are found in this delicious Greek Chicken and Pasta. It's a dish you're sure to love! To mix things up, switch the rotini for your favorite pasta.

INGREDIENTS

½ cup (about 2 ounces) rotini pasta, cooked according to package instructions

½ tablespoon olive oil

1 (6-ounce) boneless, skinless chicken breast, cut into ½" pieces

⅛ teaspoon kosher salt

⅛ teaspoon freshly ground black pepper

1 tablespoon room temperature butter

1 tablespoon peeled and chopped red onion

6 Kalamata olives, pitted

2 tablespoons crumbled feta cheese

1 tablespoon sun-dried tomatoes

1. Place cooked pasta in a medium bowl, cover, and set aside.

2. In a 10" skillet over medium heat, heat oil 30 seconds. Sprinkle all sides of chicken pieces with salt and pepper.

3. Place chicken in skillet and cook 6 minutes until all pieces are cooked through. Transfer chicken to a large plate, cover, and set aside.

4. Stir butter into pasta. Add onions, Kalamata olives, feta cheese, sun-dried tomatoes, and chicken. Toss to combine, then enjoy.

Using Sun-Dried Tomatoes

Sun-dried tomatoes make a wonderful salad topping and are also delicious in omelettes, over chicken, and in other entrées. They are often sold two ways: packed in oil or dry-packed. It's more convenient to purchase the tomatoes in oil but less expensive to purchase them dried. Both are wonderful in recipes, but the dried version will need to be rehydrated before using, as the skins are too tough to consume dry. To rehydrate sun-dried tomatoes, soak them in hot water for 10 minutes.

PER SERVING

Calories: 726   Fiber: 3g
Fat: 35g   Carbohydrates: 50g
Protein: 50g   Sugar: 3g
Sodium: 1,186mg

CHICKEN FRIED RICE

SERVES 1 | PREP: 10 MINUTES | COOK: 25 MINUTES

 This easy and flavorful dish is made with white rice, but feel free to use brown rice instead for an extra dose of fiber. It's also the perfect recipe to use when you have a little rice left over from a previous meal. Instead of chicken, consider adding shrimp or beef if you prefer. Also swap your favorite vegetables for the ones used in the recipe.

INGREDIENTS

1 (6-ounce) boneless, skinless chicken breast, cut into ½" strips.

⅛ teaspoon kosher salt

⅛ teaspoon freshly ground black pepper

½ tablespoon olive oil

½ tablespoon cold butter

½ cup peeled and chopped yellow onion

1 clove garlic, peeled and minced

¾ cup cooked white rice

1 large egg

1 cup frozen peas and carrots blend, thawed

1 tablespoon low-sodium soy sauce

1. Sprinkle all sides of chicken pieces with salt and pepper. In a 10" skillet over medium heat, heat oil 30 seconds.

2. Place chicken in skillet and cook 6 minutes until all pieces are cooked through. Transfer chicken to a large plate, cover, and set aside.

3. Add butter to skillet and melt 30 seconds. Add chopped onions and cook, stirring occasionally, 2 minutes.

4. Add minced garlic and cook, stirring occasionally, 1 minute. Then add rice and cook, stirring constantly, 30 seconds.

5. Push rice, onions, and garlic to sides of skillet. Add egg to center of skillet and stir with a spatula until egg is scrambled. When egg is almost completely cooked, stir into rice and onion mixture.

6. Add peas and carrots to skillet and cook, stirring constantly, 1 minute.

7. Add cooked chicken back to skillet and mix all ingredients together. Stir in soy sauce.

8. Scoop fried rice into a medium bowl and enjoy while hot.

PER SERVING

Calories: 691
Fat: 23g
Protein: 57g
Sodium: 1,116mg

Fiber: 8g
Carbohydrates: 62g
Sugar: 10g

CHICKEN JAMBALAYA

SERVES 1 | PREP: 15 MINUTES | COOK: 25 MINUTES

 This Chicken Jambalaya is a delicious twist on the traditional Louisiana seafood jambalaya. Made with the "holy trinity" of vegetables—green peppers, onions, and celery—this flavorful one-pot meal cooks in just 30 minutes!

INGREDIENTS

1 tablespoon olive oil, divided

1 (6-ounce) boneless, skinless chicken breast, cut into ½" cubes

½ teaspoon kosher salt, divided

¼ cup chopped green bell peppers, seeded

2 tablespoons peeled and chopped yellow onion

2 tablespoons chopped celery

1 clove garlic, peeled and minced

⅛ teaspoon cayenne pepper

½ cup canned diced tomatoes, drained

½ cup long-grain white rice

1½ cups low-sodium chicken broth

1. In a 10" skillet over medium heat, heat ½ tablespoon oil 30 seconds. Place chicken in skillet, season with ¼ teaspoon salt, and cook until chicken is browned, about 4 minutes per side.

2. Add remaining ½ tablespoon oil to skillet, then add green peppers, onions, celery, and garlic. Season with remaining salt and cayenne pepper, and cook until vegetables are soft, about 4 minutes.

3. Stir in diced tomatoes and rice and cook, stirring constantly, 1 minute.

4. Add broth and bring to a boil over high heat. Once boiling, reduce heat to medium-low, cover, and cook until rice is tender and most of the liquid is absorbed, about 25 minutes.

5. Transfer jambalaya to a medium bowl and enjoy hot.

PER SERVING

Calories: 790 Fiber: 4g
Fat: 21g Carbohydrates: 93g
Protein: 55g Sugar: 5g
Sodium: 1,371mg

BUFFALO CHICKEN SALAD

SERVES 1 | PREP: 10 MINUTES | COOK: 10 MINUTES

 Buffalo sauce is a simple mix of melted butter and hot sauce (and occasionally Worcestershire sauce and rice vinegar) that takes chicken salad to a whole new level. This salad comes together with just a few ingredients and is sure to satisfy. The chicken can also be cooked ahead of time, then added to the salad when you're ready to enjoy it. If you like your buffalo sauce to be a little spicier, add a drop or two of additional hot sauce to the recipe.

INGREDIENTS

1 tablespoon cold butter

1 (6-ounce) boneless, skinless chicken breast, cut into ½" pieces

⅛ teaspoon kosher salt

⅛ teaspoon freshly ground black pepper

½ teaspoon hot sauce

2 tablespoons chopped celery

2 tablespoons ranch dressing

2 cups chopped romaine lettuce

1. In an 8" skillet over medium heat, melt butter 30 seconds. Add chicken, season with salt and pepper, and cook until no longer pink, about 6 minutes. Transfer to a small bowl.

2. Stir in hot sauce, celery, and ranch dressing.

3. Place lettuce on a medium plate and mix in buffalo chicken. Enjoy.

PER SERVING

Calories: 454   Fiber: 2g
Fat: 30g   Carbohydrates: 5g
Protein: 40g   Sugar: 3g
Sodium: 657mg

BAKED CHICKEN TENDERS

SERVES 1 | PREP: 5 MINUTES | COOK: 20 MINUTES

 This is the *best* chicken tenders recipe! The chicken strips are dipped in melted butter, then dredged in bread crumbs, Parmesan cheese, and a flavorful mix of spices. Bakes in just 20 minutes! They are perfect by themselves or with your favorite dipping sauce.

INGREDIENTS

½ cup seasoned bread crumbs

¼ cup grated Parmesan cheese

1 teaspoon dried basil

½ teaspoon dried thyme

½ teaspoon dried oregano

½ teaspoon dried rosemary

¼ teaspoon garlic powder

¼ teaspoon kosher salt

⅛ teaspoon freshly ground black pepper

4 tablespoons (½ stick) butter, melted

8 chicken tenders

1. Preheat oven to 400°F.

2. In a small bowl, combine bread crumbs, Parmesan cheese, basil, thyme, oregano, rosemary, garlic powder, salt, and pepper. Set aside.

3. Place melted butter in a separate small bowl.

4. Dip chicken strips in melted butter, then dredge through the bread crumb mixture. Place breaded strips on a baking sheet lightly greased with butter or oil.

5. Place baking sheet in the oven and bake 20 minutes until chicken is cooked through.

6. Remove from the oven, allow to cool briefly, about 10 minutes, and eat while warm.

What Are Chicken Tenders?

Chicken tenders are an actual part of the chicken. They are the little strips of meat that are attached to the underside of a chicken breast. You can make your own by taking a boneless, skinless chicken breast and cutting it lengthwise into pieces about ½" thick, or purchase pre-packaged chicken tenders from your grocery store.

PER SERVING

Calories: 877   Fiber: 5g
Fat: 61g   Carbohydrates: 52g
Protein: 31g   Sugar: 3g
Sodium: 2,107mg

BARBECUE CHICKEN PITA PIZZA

SERVES 1 | PREP: 10 MINUTES | COOK: 15 MINUTES

 This quick and easy Barbecue Chicken Pita Pizza is savory, sweet, and cooks in just 15 minutes! Made with pita bread and cooked chicken, it makes the perfect lunch or dinner. Pita pizzas are also easily adaptable; consider swapping marinara sauce for the barbecue, adding slices of pepperoni instead of chicken, and using mozzarella cheese instead of Monterey jack for a more traditional version.

INGREDIENTS

3 tablespoons barbecue sauce, divided

1 cup chopped cooked boneless, skinless chicken breast

1 (7") whole-wheat pita bread

¼ cup shredded Monterey jack cheese

4 slices peeled red onion

1. Preheat oven to 400°F.
2. Mix 1 tablespoon barbecue sauce with cooked chicken in a small bowl.
3. Place pita bread on an ungreased baking sheet. Spread remaining 2 tablespoons barbecue sauce over top of pita.
4. Top pita with chicken and shredded cheese, then add onion.
5. Bake pizza 10 minutes.
6. Remove from oven and let sit 5 minutes, then slice and enjoy.

PER SERVING

Calories: 748
Fat: 16g
Protein: 68g
Sodium: 1,249mg

Fiber: 8g
Carbohydrates: 83g
Sugar: 26g

BARBECUE CHICKEN DRUMSTICKS

SERVES 1 | PREP: 10 MINUTES | COOK: 40 MINUTES

 These easy-to-make barbecue chicken drumsticks are baked on a bed of perfectly seasoned roasted carrots, onions, and garlic. Everything cooks in one pan for easy cleanup! Top with more barbecue sauce or your favorite dipping sauce.

INGREDIENTS

2 cups peeled and sliced carrots, cut diagonally

½ small yellow onion, peeled and rough chopped

3 cloves garlic, peeled

2 tablespoons olive oil, divided

½ teaspoon kosher salt, divided

½ teaspoon freshly ground black pepper, divided

¼ teaspoon smoked paprika

3 tablespoons barbecue sauce

3 chicken drumsticks

1. Preheat oven to 450°F.

2. Place carrots, onions, and garlic in a 9.5" baking dish lightly greased with cooking spray. Add 1 tablespoon oil, ¼ teaspoon salt, ¼ teaspoon pepper, and smoked paprika and toss to coat. Set aside.

3. In a small bowl, whisk together barbecue sauce, 1 tablespoon oil, ¼ teaspoon salt, and ¼ teaspoon pepper.

4. Place chicken drumsticks in a medium bowl and pour barbecue sauce over top. Toss, using tongs to ensure sauce mixture evenly coats each drumstick.

5. Lay chicken on top of carrots in baking dish and bake 40 minutes.

6. Remove dish from oven and cover with foil. Let rest covered 10 minutes before serving.

PER SERVING

Calories: 1,109
Fat: 65g
Protein: 76g
Sodium: 2,283mg

Fiber: 9g
Carbohydrates: 54g
Sugar: 31g

BEEF AND PORK MAIN DISHES

Beef and pork can seem like they are at opposite ends of the food spectrum: Beef is often considered heavy and hearty, while pork is seen as "the other white meat." In truth, both meats can be either lean or hearty depending on the cut purchased. Buying a great cut of beef or pork also becomes a lot easier and economical when you are cooking for one; you can ask the butcher to sell you one piece from the counter, or purchase a package of meat to divide up and freeze for later. Either way, you won't have to skimp on quality.

Whether you consider yourself a meat and potatoes type of person, or someone who prefers a lighter option for dinner, you'll find new favorite recipes in this chapter. Beef recipes include Classic Meatloaf, Mediterranean Meatball Pitas with Tzatziki Sauce, and Salisbury Steak. And when on sale, you can pick up a single tenderloin for as little as a few dollars to enjoy in the Beef Fajitas! Then, as you work your way through different pork recipes, you'll quickly realize just how flavorful and versatile this meat is. The Sweet and Spicy Pork Lettuce Wraps and Pasta with Pork Ragù provide two distinct, easy approaches you'll love. You will also find a recipe for the most tender and juicy Oven-Baked Pork Chop you've ever had (a real favorite of mine). So let's get cooking!

BEEF STEW

SERVES 1 | PREP: 20 MINUTES | COOK: 80 MINUTES

One tip for making the best stew every time is to sear the meat before slow-cooking in your pot with the remaining ingredients. Searing first traps in the meat's flavors.

INGREDIENTS

1 tablespoon canola oil, divided

8 ounces beef chuck roast, cut into 1" cubes

¼ teaspoon kosher salt

⅛ teaspoon freshly ground black pepper

½ cup peeled and chopped yellow onion

1 medium stalk celery, chopped

1 clove garlic, peeled and minced

½ tablespoon tomato paste

½ tablespoon Worcestershire sauce

1 tablespoon all-purpose flour

¼ cup dry red wine

½ teaspoon dried thyme

2 cups low-sodium chicken broth

1 small yellow potato, scrubbed and cubed

1 small carrot, peeled and cut into ½" slices

¼ cup frozen peas

1. In a 10" skillet or small Dutch oven over medium-high heat, heat ½ tablespoon canola oil 30 seconds. Season meat with salt and pepper, then add to skillet and brown on all sides, about 10 minutes total.

2. Remove beef from skillet and place on a medium plate. Set aside.

3. Add ½ tablespoon canola oil to skillet and stir in chopped onions and celery. Cook, stirring occasionally, until onions are translucent, about 10 minutes.

4. Add garlic and cook until fragrant, about 30 seconds. Stir in tomato paste and Worcestershire sauce.

5. Sprinkle flour over vegetables. Stir until there is no visible flour and vegetables look slightly mushy, about 3 minutes.

6. Pour in wine and thyme. Stir until wine has reduced and thickens slightly, about 3 minutes.

7. Add broth and return meat to skillet. Cover and reduce heat to low. Simmer 25 minutes, stirring occasionally.

8. Add potatoes and carrots. Cover again and continue cooking an additional 25 minutes. When done, meat should be tender and flake apart easily, and potatoes cooked through. If not, cover and cook in additional 15-minute increments until fully cooked.

9. Stir in peas, then spoon stew into a medium bowl. Enjoy.

PER SERVING

Calories: 957
Fat: 48g
Protein: 65g
Sodium: 993mg

Fiber: 8g
Carbohydrates: 66g
Sugar: 11g

BEEF STROGANOFF

SERVES 1 | PREP: 10 MINUTES | COOK: 30 MINUTES

 This Beef Stroganoff features tender beef smothered in a rich and creamy mushroom sauce, served over buttered noodles. It's a one-pot meal that feels fancy but is so easy to make and is the ultimate comfort food! Enjoy with a slice of warm, crusty bread.

INGREDIENTS

2½ tablespoons butter, divided

8 ounces beef sirloin steak, thinly sliced

¼ teaspoon kosher salt

⅛ teaspoon freshly ground black pepper

1 cup peeled and chopped yellow onion

1 clove garlic, peeled and minced

½ cup sliced white mushrooms

¼ cup dry white wine

½ cup beef broth

1 teaspoon Worcestershire sauce

1 tablespoon all-purpose flour

¼ cup plain full-fat yogurt

1 cup uncooked wide egg noodles

1. In a 10" skillet over medium heat, melt 1 tablespoon butter 30 seconds.

2. Season both sides of beef with salt and pepper. Add beef in a single layer to skillet and cook until browned, about 3 minutes per side.

3. Remove beef from skillet and transfer to a medium plate.

4. Add 1 tablespoon butter to skillet and melt 30 seconds. Add chopped onions and cook 3 minutes, stirring occasionally. Add garlic and mushrooms and cook an additional 6 minutes until mushrooms are softened, continuing to stir occasionally.

5. Stir in white wine and cook 3 minutes.

6. While mushroom mixture is cooking, whisk together beef broth, Worcestershire sauce, and flour in a medium bowl. Pour into skillet.

7. Bring to a simmer over medium heat and cook 5 minutes, stirring occasionally. Stir in yogurt.

8. While mixture simmers, cook noodles over high heat in a medium pot of boiling water until tender, about 8 minutes.

9. Drain noodles, then transfer to a medium plate. Toss with remaining butter. Top with beef, then mushroom sauce. Enjoy.

PER SERVING

Calories: 843
Fat: 39g
Protein: 61g
Sodium: 1,205mg

Fiber: 5g
Carbohydrates: 55g
Sugar: 12g

VEGETABLE BEEF SOUP

SERVES 1 | PREP: 15 MINUTES | COOK: 45 MINUTES

 This hearty Vegetable Beef Soup is filled with fresh vegetables and chunks of tender beef. The recipe calls for using beef stew meat, but you can also use sirloin. Be sure to sear the meat first for a good 2 minutes before adding to the remaining ingredients. You will know when the meat is well-seared when the sides have a dark crust.

INGREDIENTS

1 tablespoon olive oil

¼ pound beef stew meat, cut into 1" cubes

¼ teaspoon kosher salt, divided

⅛ teaspoon freshly ground black pepper

½ cup peeled and chopped yellow onion

¼ cup chopped, seeded green peppers

1 medium stalk celery, chopped

1 small carrot, peeled and chopped

1 clove garlic, peeled and minced

½ cup fresh green beans

½ tablespoon Worcestershire sauce

¼ teaspoon dried thyme

¼ teaspoon steak seasoning

1 small yellow potato, peeled and cubed

1½ cups beef broth

1. In a 2-quart pot over medium-high heat, heat oil 30 seconds. Season beef with ⅛ teaspoon salt and pepper and add to pot.

2. Sear beef 2 minutes on each side until browned. Transfer cooked beef to a large plate and set aside.

3. Add onions, green peppers, celery, carrots, garlic, green beans, and remaining salt to pot. Cook, stirring frequently, until vegetables soften, about 5 minutes.

4. Stir in Worcestershire, thyme, steak seasoning, and potatoes. Cook 1 minute, stirring occasionally.

5. Pour broth into pot, along with beef, and bring to a boil over high heat. Once boiling, cover, reduce heat to low, and simmer 30 minutes.

6. Transfer to a medium plate and enjoy.

PER SERVING

Calories: 635
Fat: 30g
Protein: 44g
Sodium: 2,651mg

Fiber: 8g
Carbohydrates: 48g
Sugar: 11g

SPANISH RICE

SERVES 1 | PREP: 5 MINUTES | COOK: 25 MINUTES

 Filled with onions, bell peppers, garlic, tomatoes, and beef, this Spanish Rice is a delicious, hearty recipe that can be ready in under 30 minutes! If you like your rice spicy, add a few drops of hot sauce after it's cooked.

INGREDIENTS

½ tablespoon olive oil

2 tablespoons peeled and chopped yellow onion

2 tablespoons chopped, seeded green bell peppers

1 clove garlic, peeled and minced

¼ teaspoon kosher salt, divided

⅛ teaspoon freshly ground black pepper

4 ounces ground beef

½ cup canned diced tomatoes, including juice

½ cup long-grain white rice

1½ cups chicken broth

1. In a 10" skillet over medium-high heat, heat oil 30 seconds. Add onions, bell peppers, garlic, ⅛ teaspoon salt, and pepper and cook, stirring occasionally, 3 minutes.

2. Add ground beef and cook, stirring frequently, until beef is cooked, about 5 minutes.

3. Stir in tomatoes, rice, chicken broth, and remaining salt. Bring to a boil over high heat, then reduce heat to low, cover, and simmer 25 minutes until rice is tender and most liquid is absorbed.

4. Spoon into a medium bowl and enjoy immediately.

PER SERVING

Calories: 753
Fat: 26g
Protein: 34g
Sodium: 2,194mg

Fiber: 4g
Carbohydrates: 95g
Sugar: 9g

BROCCOLINI WITH SAUSAGE

SERVES 1 | PREP: 10 MINUTES | COOK: 15 MINUTES

 Easy, healthy, and absolutely delicious, this Broccolini with Sausage meal is perfect for a busy evening. Steamed Broccolini (a crossbreed of broccoli and Chinese broccoli) are sautéed in oil with sliced garlic and sausage. Enjoy over rice or by itself. This wonderful recipe can be on your table in 30 minutes!

INGREDIENTS

¼ pound Broccolini

1 tablespoon olive oil

1 (4-ounce) smoked Italian sausage link, sliced in half lengthwise

1 clove garlic, peeled and sliced

⅛ teaspoon red pepper flakes

½ tablespoon lemon juice

2 tablespoons shredded Parmesan cheese

1. Boil Broccolini in a medium pot of salted water over high heat 2 minutes. Drain immediately and cool under cold running water. Gently squeeze Broccolini and pat dry with a towel. Place on a cutting board and chop. Set aside.

2. In a 10" skillet over medium-high heat, heat oil 30 seconds. Add sausages and cook one side 2 minutes.

3. Flip sausages over, add garlic and red pepper flakes and cook other side an additional 2 minutes, stirring occasionally so garlic doesn't burn.

4. Add Broccolini and cook, stirring until tender, about 3 minutes.

5. Remove skillet from heat, and stir in lemon juice and Parmesan cheese. Transfer to a medium plate and enjoy immediately.

PER SERVING

Calories: 570
Fat: 49g
Protein: 21g
Sodium: 1,234mg

Fiber: 5g
Carbohydrates: 10g
Sugar: 2g

SALISBURY STEAK

SERVES 1 | PREP: 10 MINUTES | COOK: 20 MINUTES

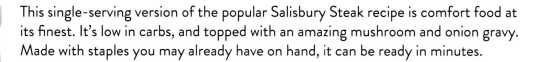

This single-serving version of the popular Salisbury Steak recipe is comfort food at its finest. It's low in carbs, and topped with an amazing mushroom and onion gravy. Made with staples you may already have on hand, it can be ready in minutes.

INGREDIENTS

For Beef Patty

8 ounces ground beef

½ teaspoon Worcestershire sauce

½ teaspoon Italian seasoning

¼ teaspoon mustard powder

¼ teaspoon garlic powder

⅛ teaspoon kosher salt

⅛ teaspoon freshly ground black pepper

½ tablespoon olive oil

For Gravy

½ tablespoon butter

¼ small yellow onion, peeled and thinly sliced

¼ cup sliced white mushrooms

½ teaspoon Worcestershire sauce

½ cup beef broth

1 teaspoon sour cream

1. **To make Beef Patty:** Mix together ground beef, Worcestershire sauce, Italian seasoning, mustard powder, garlic powder, salt, and pepper in a medium bowl.

2. Flatten beef into a round patty, about ½" thick.

3. In a 10" skillet over medium heat, heat oil 30 seconds. Add beef patty and cook 4 minutes per side until patty is no longer rare.

4. Remove patty from skillet and place on a large plate. Cover with aluminum foil and set aside.

1. **To make Gravy:** Reduce heat to medium-low and add butter to skillet. Melt butter 30 seconds, then add onions and cook, stirring occasionally, 3 minutes.

2. Add mushrooms and cook, stirring occasionally, until mushrooms have softened, about 3 minutes.

3. Stir in Worcestershire sauce and beef broth, bring mixture to a gentle boil over medium-high heat, stirring occasionally, then reduce heat to low. Simmer 3 minutes.

4. Stir in sour cream. Add patty back to skillet and cook 1 minute, spooning some gravy over meat as it cooks.

5. Remove beef patty from pan and place on a medium plate. Pour gravy over top and enjoy.

PER SERVING

Calories: 640
Fat: 48g
Protein: 45g
Sodium: 947mg

Fiber: 1g
Carbohydrates: 6g
Sugar: 2g

CLASSIC MEATLOAF

SERVES 1 | PREP: 15 MINUTES | COOK: 50 MINUTES

 If you've been scarred by memories of dry, tasteless meatloaf from your childhood days, it might be time for you to revisit this classic—the right way. This single-serving Classic Meatloaf is tender and juicy and so easy to make! It might just become your new favorite meal.

INGREDIENTS

1 tablespoon olive oil

2 tablespoons peeled and chopped yellow onion

1 clove garlic, peeled and minced

¼ teaspoon dried basil

6 ounces ground beef

¼ teaspoon kosher salt

⅛ teaspoon freshly ground black pepper

¼ teaspoon Worcestershire sauce

1 large egg, beaten

2 tablespoons seasoned bread crumbs

2 tablespoons ketchup

½ tablespoon molasses

1. Preheat oven to 350°F.

2. In an 8" skillet over medium heat, heat oil 30 seconds. Add onions and cook 2 minutes.

3. Add garlic and dried basil. Cook, stirring occasionally, an additional 2 minutes. Remove skillet from heat and set aside.

4. Place ground beef in a medium bowl. Pour onion mixture over meat. Add salt, pepper, Worcestershire sauce, egg, and bread crumbs, using a large spoon to mix until ingredients are fully combined.

5. Shape mixture into an oval and place in a 5" × 5" baking dish lightly greased with butter or oil. Bake 30 minutes.

6. In a small separate bowl, whisk together ketchup and molasses. Pour over top of meatloaf.

7. Return meatloaf to oven and bake an additional 20 minutes.

8. Remove from oven and cover with aluminum foil. Let rest 10 minutes before eating.

PER SERVING

Calories: 692   *Fiber: 1g*
Fat: 45g   *Carbohydrates: 31g*
Protein: 41g   *Sugar: 17g*
Sodium: 1,293mg

STUFFED PEPPER

SERVES 1 | PREP: 15 MINUTES | COOK: 20 MINUTES

 Stuffed peppers are such an easy meal to make. I've kept this recipe simple by filling a single-serving pepper with lean ground beef, vegetables, and Cheddar cheese, but you can fill it with any combination of meats, beans, sauces, and cheeses you prefer.

INGREDIENTS

1 medium green bell pepper, top removed, seeded, and cut in half lengthwise

¼ teaspoon kosher salt, divided

1 tablespoon olive oil

¼ cup peeled and chopped yellow onion

1 clove garlic, peeled and minced

4 ounces ground beef

¼ teaspoon dried basil

¼ teaspoon dried oregano

⅛ teaspoon freshly ground black pepper

¼ cup canned diced tomatoes, drained

3 tablespoons shredded Cheddar cheese, divided

1. Preheat oven to 375°F.

2. Fill a small pot with water and bring to a boil over high heat. Immerse pepper halves in boiling water 3 minutes.

3. Carefully remove peppers from water and place on a paper towel. Sprinkle insides with ⅛ teaspoon salt, then invert on paper towel to drain well.

4. In a 10" skillet over medium heat, heat oil 30 seconds. Add onions and cook 2 minutes, stirring occasionally. Add garlic and cook an additional 2 minutes.

5. Add ground beef to skillet and season with basil, oregano, remaining salt, and pepper. Cook until browned, about 5 minutes.

6. Pour in diced tomatoes; reduce heat to medium-low, and simmer 5 minutes.

7. Remove skillet from heat and stir in 2 tablespoons Cheddar cheese. Spoon mixture into pepper halves.

8. Stand peppers in a 5" × 5" baking dish lightly greased with butter or oil. Sprinkle remaining cheese over peppers.

9. Cover dish with aluminum foil and bake 15 minutes. Enjoy immediately.

PER SERVING

Calories: 528
Fat: 38g
Protein: 29g
Sodium: 807mg

Fiber: 5g
Carbohydrates: 17g
Sugar: 9g

ITALIAN WEDDING SOUP

SERVES 1 | PREP: 10 MINUTES | COOK: 20 MINUTES

 My grandmother used to make Italian Wedding Soup when I was a little girl, and although I loved it, I was hesitant to make it because I always assumed it was a chore to make the meatballs before making the soup itself. This recipe proves I was wrong all those years! The soup is actually very easy to make, and can be ready in 30 minutes. Enjoy topped with additional Parmesan cheese.

INGREDIENTS

4 ounces ground beef

2 cloves garlic, peeled and minced, divided

¼ teaspoon kosher salt

⅛ teaspoon freshly ground black pepper

1 tablespoon chopped fresh parsley

1 tablespoon grated Parmesan cheese

½ tablespoon olive oil

¼ cup peeled and chopped yellow onion

1 small carrot, peeled and chopped

2 cups low-sodium chicken broth

⅓ cup fresh spinach, packed down and roughly chopped

¼ cup orzo pasta, uncooked

1. In a medium bowl, combine ground beef, 1 clove garlic, salt, pepper, parsley, and Parmesan cheese. Shape mixture into 1" mini meatballs and set aside.

2. In a 3-quart pot over medium-high heat, heat oil 30 seconds. Add onions and carrots and cook until tender, about 3 minutes. Add remaining garlic and cook, stirring occasionally, an additional minute.

3. Add meatballs and chicken broth to pot, then stir in spinach and pasta.

4. Bring mixture to a boil over high heat, then reduce heat to medium-low and simmer 15 minutes until meatballs and pasta are fully cooked.

5. Ladle soup into a medium bowl and enjoy.

PER SERVING

Calories: 627
Fat: 29g
Protein: 41g
Sodium: 1,514mg

Fiber: 4g
Carbohydrates: 53g
Sugar: 7g

PASTA WITH PORK RAGÙ

SERVES 1 | PREP: 10 MINUTES | COOK: 25 MINUTES

 This Pasta with Pork Ragù is sometimes referred to as "goulash" or "DIY Hamburger Helper." It's a wonderfully easy meal to throw together, and many of the ingredients are staples you may already have in your pantry. This recipe also allows for plenty of flexibility, so feel free to add in different seasonal vegetables you have on hand.

INGREDIENTS

½ tablespoon olive oil

¼ cup peeled and chopped yellow onion

1 small carrot, peeled and finely chopped

1 clove garlic, peeled and minced

4 ounces ground pork

¼ teaspoon kosher salt

⅛ teaspoon freshly ground black pepper

¼ teaspoon dried oregano

1 (14-ounce) can diced tomatoes, including juice

2 ounces elbow macaroni, cooked according to instructions

½ tablespoon shredded Parmesan cheese

1. In a 10" skillet over medium-high heat, heat oil 30 seconds. Add onions and carrots and cook, stirring occasionally, 4 minutes until carrots soften.

2. Add garlic, pork, salt, pepper, and oregano to skillet and cook, stirring frequently, 4 minutes until pork is browned.

3. Add diced tomatoes and bring to a boil over high heat, then reduce heat to low and simmer 15 minutes, stirring occasionally.

4. Add cooked pasta and stir to coat. Top with Parmesan cheese.

5. Transfer to a medium bowl and enjoy hot.

PER SERVING

Calories: 696
Fat: 27g
Protein: 37g
Sodium: 1,639mg

Fiber: 12g
Carbohydrates: 81g
Sugar: 22g

OVEN-BAKED PORK CHOP

SERVES 1 | PREP: 5 MINUTES | COOK: 15 MINUTES

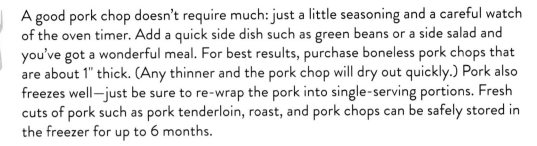

A good pork chop doesn't require much: just a little seasoning and a careful watch of the oven timer. Add a quick side dish such as green beans or a side salad and you've got a wonderful meal. For best results, purchase boneless pork chops that are about 1" thick. (Any thinner and the pork chop will dry out quickly.) Pork also freezes well—just be sure to re-wrap the pork into single-serving portions. Fresh cuts of pork such as pork tenderloin, roast, and pork chops can be safely stored in the freezer for up to 6 months.

INGREDIENTS

½ tablespoon olive oil

1 boneless pork chop, ½" thick

¼ teaspoon kosher salt

¼ teaspoon smoked paprika

¼ teaspoon garlic powder

⅛ teaspoon freshly ground black pepper

1. Preheat oven to 400°F. Lightly grease a small baking sheet with butter or oil.

2. Rub oil over pork chop. Set aside.

3. In a small bowl, mix together salt, smoked paprika, garlic powder, and black pepper. Sprinkle over both sides of pork.

4. Place pork on baking sheet and bake 15 minutes, or until pork chop reaches an internal temperature of 145°F.

5. Remove from oven, cover, and let rest 10 minutes before eating.

Tips for Cooking Pork Chops

To guarantee tender and juicy pork chops every single time, first be sure to season the pork before cooking to enhance the texture and taste. Second, do not cook the pork straight from the refrigerator. Instead, remove it from the refrigerator 10 minutes before you are ready to cook it, so it cooks more evenly. Third, follow the cook times in this recipe to avoid overcooking. And finally, let the pork rest for 10 minutes after cooking. This gives you a juicier, more tender piece of meat.

PER SERVING

Calories: 285

Fat: 20g

Protein: 24g

Sodium: 635mg

Fiber: 0g

Carbohydrates: 1g

Sugar: 0g

BEEF FAJITAS

SERVES 1 | PREP: 10 MINUTES | COOK: 15 MINUTES

 Fajitas are such an easy and adaptable dish to make. Consider topping yours with shredded cheese, chopped cilantro, and a dollop of sour cream. For a low-carb option, enjoy the cooked steak and vegetables over a plate of chopped salad greens: truly spectacular!

INGREDIENTS

4 ounces boneless beef sirloin steak, cut into thin strips

¼ teaspoon steak seasoning

1 tablespoon olive oil, divided

½ small yellow onion, peeled and sliced

½ small green bell pepper, seeded and cut into thin strips

2 (8") flour tortillas

1. Toss steak strips with seasoning in a small bowl. Set aside.

2. In a 10" skillet over medium-high heat, heat ½ tablespoon oil 30 seconds. Add beef and cook, stirring occasionally, 5 minutes until beef is no longer pink.

3. Remove beef from skillet and place on a large plate. Cover and set aside.

4. Add remaining ½ tablespoon oil to skillet. Add onions and peppers and cook, stirring frequently, 5 minutes until vegetables have softened.

5. Return meat to the pan and stir until heated through, about 1 minute, then spoon mixture onto tortillas. Enjoy immediately.

PER SERVING

Calories: 604
Fat: 24g
Protein: 33g
Sodium: 628mg

Fiber: 5g
Carbohydrates: 63g
Sugar: 4g

SAUSAGE AND PEPPERS SHEET PAN MEAL

SERVES 1 | PREP: 10 MINUTES | COOK: 20 MINUTES

 This savory, simple Sausage and Peppers Sheet Pan Meal can be ready in under 30 minutes! Although this recipe uses Italian sausage, feel free to use just about any type of smoked sausage you like. Great options include kielbasa, andouille, bratwurst, turkey sausage, and chicken sausage.

INGREDIENTS

1 (3.5-ounce) Italian sausage link, sliced

1 medium red bell pepper, seeded and sliced

¼ small Vidalia onion, peeled and sliced

½ tablespoon olive oil

⅛ teaspoon kosher salt

⅛ teaspoon freshly ground black pepper

1. Preheat oven to 400°F.

2. Spread sausage on a small ungreased baking sheet. Add peppers and onions to pan.

3. Drizzle oil over tops of sausage and vegetables, then sprinkle with salt and pepper.

4. Toss sausage and vegetables until evenly coated with oil, salt, and pepper.

5. Place pan in oven and bake 20 minutes. Enjoy immediately.

PER SERVING

Calories: 252

Fat: 15g

Protein: 17g

Sodium: 862mg

Fiber: 3g

Carbohydrates: 11g

Sugar: 6g

VEGETABLE AND PORK BOWL

SERVES 1 | PREP: 10 MINUTES | COOK: 15 MINUTES

 Here's a pork stir-fry recipe that's easy to make and filled with flavor. Ground pork is seasoned perfectly and cooked with vegetables, served in a terrific sauce over rice. Ready in under 30 minutes, this delightful single-serving recipe needs to be on your dinner menu.

INGREDIENTS

1 teaspoon olive oil

4 ounces ground pork

⅛ teaspoon kosher salt

¼ cup sliced white mushrooms

¼ cup peeled and chopped yellow onion

1 small carrot, peeled and chopped

1 clove garlic, peeled and minced

⅛ teaspoon ground ginger

1 cup spinach, loosely packed

1 tablespoon low-sodium soy sauce

½ teaspoon apple cider vinegar

⅛ teaspoon freshly ground black pepper

1 cup cooked white rice

1. In a 10" skillet over medium-high heat, heat oil 30 seconds. Add pork and salt and cook, stirring frequently, until completely cooked, about 4 minutes. Transfer pork to a large bowl and set aside.

2. Add mushrooms, onions, and carrots to skillet. Cook, stirring occasionally, 2 minutes. Add garlic and ginger and cook, stirring constantly, 30 seconds.

3. Stir in spinach, soy sauce, vinegar, and pepper. Cook, stirring constantly, until the spinach wilts, about 30 seconds.

4. Pour into bowl with pork, then pour contents over cooked rice in a large serving dish. Enjoy.

How to Bake a Single Serving of Rice

For an individual helping of rice, simply add ¼ cup rice, ¾ cup water, ¼ tablespoon butter, and ⅛ teaspoon kosher salt to an oven-safe ramekin or 5" × 5" baking dish. Preheat your oven to 325°F, then bake the rice for 40 minutes until the water is absorbed and the rice is tender.

PER SERVING

Calories: 546

Fat: 22g

Protein: 29g

Sodium: 981mg

Fiber: 4g

Carbohydrates: 57g

Sugar: 5g

CRUSTLESS GOAT CHEESE AND PROSCIUTTO QUICHE

SERVES 1 | PREP: 10 MINUTES | COOK: 25 MINUTES

 Easy to make and low in carbs, this Crustless Goat Cheese and Prosciutto Quiche is a delicious combination of flavors. When it bakes in the oven, it forms a "natural" crust, so you don't need to spend the extra time making your own crust.

INGREDIENTS

½ tablespoon room temperature butter

2 large eggs

4 tablespoons heavy cream

⅛ teaspoon garlic powder

⅛ teaspoon kosher salt

⅛ teaspoon freshly ground black pepper

1 ounce (about ¼ cup) chopped prosciutto

¼ cup crumbled goat cheese

2 tablespoons chopped green onion

1 Preheat oven to 400°F and lightly grease inside of a 5" × 5" baking dish with butter.

2 In a medium mixing bowl, whisk together eggs, cream, garlic powder, salt, and pepper.

3 Stir in chopped prosciutto, goat cheese, and green onions.

4 Pour mixture into baking dish and bake 25 minutes until quiche is puffed and golden. Enjoy immediately.

PER SERVING

Calories: 585
Fat: 49g
Protein: 31g
Sodium: 1,367mg

Fiber: 0g
Carbohydrates: 4g
Sugar: 3g

PORK AND ZUCCHINI STIR-FRY

SERVES 1 | PREP: 10 MINUTES | COOK: 20 MINUTES

 Stir-fries are great because they are easy to make and can be well-balanced, satisfying meals. Eat this single-serving version over rice, or enjoy it on its own for a low-carb meal.

INGREDIENTS

For Sauce

2 tablespoons low-sodium soy sauce

1 teaspoon olive oil

½ teaspoon Asian chili sauce

⅛ teaspoon ground ginger

For Stir-Fry

½ tablespoon olive oil

5 ounces ground pork

⅛ teaspoon kosher salt

⅛ teaspoon freshly ground black pepper

1 small zucchini, diced

1. **To make Sauce:** In a small bowl, whisk together soy sauce, oil, chili sauce, and ginger. Set aside.

1. **To make Stir-Fry:** In a 10" skillet over medium-high heat, heat oil 30 seconds. Add pork and season with salt and pepper. Cook, stirring occasionally, 4 minutes until browned.

2. Transfer cooked pork to a large paper towel–lined plate and set aside.

3. Add zucchini to skillet and spread out into one even layer. Cook 30 seconds, then flip over and cook until browned and just tender, about 3 minutes.

4. Return pork to skillet and add sauce. Cook until sauce is well incorporated, about 30 seconds, then spoon onto a medium plate and enjoy.

PER SERVING

Calories: 466   Fiber: 1g
Fat: 33g   Carbohydrates: 8g
Protein: 30g   Sugar: 4g
Sodium: 1,569mg

SWEET AND SPICY PORK LETTUCE WRAPS

SERVES 1 | PREP: 10 MINUTES | COOK: 15 MINUTES

 A quick and healthy meal, pork lettuce wraps are incredibly easy to make and full of flavor. The secret to making these lettuce wraps so tasty is in the Asian chili sauce—a sweet and spicy sauce that can be found in the ethnic foods aisle of most supermarkets. Keep a jar in your refrigerator to add to burgers, seafood, and chicken.

INGREDIENTS

½ tablespoon olive oil

2 tablespoons peeled and chopped yellow onion

2 tablespoons chopped, seeded red peppers

1 clove garlic, peeled and minced

5 ounces ground pork

⅛ teaspoon kosher salt

⅛ teaspoon freshly ground black pepper

1 teaspoon Asian chili sauce

2 Bibb lettuce leaves

1. In a 10" skillet over medium-high heat, heat oil 30 seconds. Add onions and red peppers and cook, stirring occasionally, until onions soften, about 3 minutes. Add garlic and cook an additional minute.

2. Add pork and season with salt and pepper. Cook until pork is no longer pink, about 4 minutes. Stir in chili sauce and cook, stirring frequently, another 2 minutes.

3. Spoon pork mixture into lettuce leaves on a medium plate. Enjoy warm.

PER SERVING

Calories: 397   Fiber: 1g
Fat: 28g   Carbohydrates: 9g
Protein: 27g   Sugar: 4g
Sodium: 456mg

SAUSAGE AND PEPPER HOAGIE

SERVES 1 | PREP: 10 MINUTES | COOK: 15 MINUTES

 Sizzling hot sausage and sweet bell peppers are piled high on top of a soft hoagie roll. Consider enjoying this delightful sandwich with a side of sauerkraut and stone-ground mustard for dipping.

INGREDIENTS

1 tablespoon olive oil, divided

5 ounces mild Italian sausage links, sliced in half lengthwise

1 small red pepper, thinly sliced and seeded

¼ small Vidalia onion, peeled and thinly sliced

⅛ teaspoon kosher salt

⅛ teaspoon freshly ground black pepper

⅛ teaspoon dried basil

1 hoagie roll

1 In a 10" skillet over medium-high heat, heat ½ tablespoon oil 30 seconds. Place both halves of sausage in skillet and cook 3 minutes on each side. Transfer sausage to a large plate and set aside.

2 Add remaining oil to skillet. Add sliced peppers, onions, salt, pepper, and basil and cook, stirring occasionally, 4 minutes until vegetables soften.

3 Place sausage on roll and top with vegetables. Enjoy.

PER SERVING

Calories: 565   Fiber: 5g
Fat: 32g   Carbohydrates: 44g
Protein: 24g   Sugar: 7g
Sodium: 1,352mg

SPICY SAUSAGE PASTA

SERVES 1 | PREP: 10 MINUTES | COOK: 25 MINUTES

 A scaled-down version of a sausage and pasta dish I used to make when my children were young, this delicious pasta dish is comfort food at its finest. It is quick to make, filled with flavor, and completely satisfying.

INGREDIENTS

½ tablespoon olive oil

5 ounces smoked sausage, sliced

¼ cup peeled and chopped yellow onion

1 clove garlic, peeled and minced

1 medium Roma tomato, chopped

½ cup low-sodium chicken broth

2 tablespoons heavy cream

⅛ teaspoon kosher salt

⅛ teaspoon freshly ground black pepper

2 ounces egg noodles

¼ cup Monterey jack cheese

1. In a 10" skillet over medium-high heat, heat oil 30 seconds. Add sausage and onions and cook until sausage is lightly browned, about 4 minutes. Add garlic and cook an additional 30 seconds.

2. Add tomatoes and cook, stirring constantly, 30 seconds. Pour in chicken broth and cream, then stir in salt, pepper, and noodles.

3. Bring mixture to a boil over high heat, then reduce heat to low, cover, and simmer 15 minutes until pasta is tender and sauce has thickened.

4. Remove skillet from heat and stir in cheese, then transfer to a medium plate and serve hot.

PER SERVING

Calories: 990

Fat: 70g

Protein: 36g

Sodium: 1,522mg

Fiber: 3g

Carbohydrates: 54g

Sugar: 6g

PETITE FILET WITH MUSHROOM SAUCE

SERVES 1 | PREP: 15 MINUTES | COOK: 20 MINUTES

 The only thing this meal needs is candlelight and a wonderful glass of wine. A tender and juicy filet is quickly seared in a skillet, then transferred to the oven to finish cooking. Meanwhile, a mouthwatering sauce is prepared on the stove and then poured over the cooked steak. It's a gourmet meal that is also incredibly easy to make.

INGREDIENTS

For Filet

½ tablespoon olive oil

1 (6-ounce) filet of beef, about 1" thick

⅛ teaspoon kosher salt

⅛ teaspoon freshly ground black pepper

For Sauce

1 tablespoon olive oil

½ cup sliced white mushrooms

1 tablespoon peeled and chopped yellow onion

¼ teaspoon dried thyme

⅛ teaspoon kosher salt

¼ cup dry white wine

3 tablespoons blue cheese crumbles

1 tablespoon mayonnaise

½ tablespoon Dijon mustard

PER SERVING

Calories: 633   Fiber: 1g
Fat: 48g   Carbohydrates: 4g
Protein: 41g   Sugar: 2g
Sodium: 1,094mg

1. **To make Filet:** Preheat oven to 400°F.

2. In a small skillet over medium-high heat, heat oil 30 seconds. Sprinkle both sides of beef with salt and pepper.

3. Place beef in skillet and sear on both sides, about 4 minutes per side.

4. Transfer steak (still in skillet) to oven and bake 5 minutes. Remove steak when a meat thermometer inserted in the center reads 125°F (for medium rare) or 130°F (for medium).

5. Cover steak with aluminum foil and let rest for 5 minutes.

1. **To make Sauce:** While steak is resting, heat oil in a separate small skillet over medium heat 30 seconds. Add mushrooms and onions and cook until onions are golden brown and tender, about 4 minutes.

2. Add thyme, salt, and white wine to skillet, and continue cooking, stirring occasionally, until liquid has evaporated, about 5 minutes.

3. Meanwhile, combine blue cheese crumbles, mayonnaise, and mustard in a small bowl. Transfer to skillet with mushrooms and gently stir.

4. Spoon sauce over beef and enjoy.

BEEF CHILI

SERVES 1 | PREP: 10 MINUTES | COOK: 25 MINUTES

 This hearty Beef Chili is loaded with vegetables and beans and can be ready in just 30 minutes. It's a classic recipe perfect for a busy weeknight. Consider topping your bowl of chili with shredded cheese, sliced jalapeños, sour cream, and chopped cilantro.

INGREDIENTS

1 tablespoon olive oil

½ cup peeled and chopped yellow onion

½ cup chopped and seeded red bell peppers

1 clove garlic, peeled and minced

4 ounces ground beef

¼ teaspoon chili powder

¼ teaspoon ground cumin

½ teaspoon kosher salt

¼ cup canned red beans, rinsed and drained

1 (15-ounce) can diced tomatoes, including juice

½ teaspoon dried basil

1. In a 10" skillet over medium heat, heat oil 30 seconds. Add onions and peppers and cook, stirring occasionally, 2 minutes. Stir in garlic and cook an additional 1 minute.

2. Add ground beef to skillet and break up with a spatula. Stir occasionally and cook until no longer pink, about 8 minutes.

3. Add chili powder, cumin, and salt; stir another 10 seconds.

4. Add beans, tomatoes, and basil, then bring mixture to a boil over high heat. Once boiling, reduce heat to a simmer on low heat and cook 10 minutes.

5. Spoon chili into a medium bowl and enjoy hot.

PER SERVING

Calories: 612	Fiber: 14g
Fat: 33g	Carbohydrates: 53g
Protein: 33g	Sugar: 25g
Sodium: 2,138mg	

MEDITERRANEAN MEATBALL PITAS WITH TZATZIKI SAUCE

SERVES 1 | PREP: 15 MINUTES | COOK: 20 MINUTES

These tender and juicy meatballs are filled with popular Mediterranean ingredients such as Kalamata olives, sun-dried tomatoes, and feta cheese. They bake in 20 minutes and are stuffed into a whole-wheat pita for a boost of fiber.

INGREDIENTS

For Meatballs

4 ounces ground beef

1 clove garlic, peeled and minced

¼ teaspoon kosher salt

⅛ teaspoon ground black pepper

3 Kalamata olives, chopped

1 tablespoon chopped sun-dried tomatoes

1 tablespoon crumbled feta cheese

For Sauce

½ medium cucumber, peeled and sliced

¼ cup plain Greek yogurt

1 clove garlic, peeled and minced

1 tablespoon olive oil

½ tablespoon lemon juice

½ teaspoon fresh mint leaves

⅛ teaspoon kosher salt

For Pita

1 (6") whole-wheat pita, sliced in half

2 slices vine-ripe tomato

¼ cup fresh spinach leaves

1. **To make Meatballs:** Preheat oven to 400°F. Line a baking sheet with foil and lightly grease foil with cooking spray.

2. In a medium bowl, stir together beef, garlic, salt, pepper, olives, sun-dried tomatoes, and feta cheese.

3. Shape beef mixture into 1 tablespoon-sized meatballs and place on prepared baking sheet.

4. Bake 20 minutes until meatballs are no longer pink inside.

1. **To make Tzatziki Sauce:** Place cucumber, yogurt, garlic, oil, lemon juice, mint, and salt in a blender. Cover and pulse until smooth.

1. **To make Pita:** Add 1 tablespoon sauce to bottom of each pita half. Add tomatoes and spinach. Divide meatballs into pita halves and pour remaining sauce on top. Enjoy.

PER SERVING

Calories: 708
Fat: 40g
Protein: 36g
Sodium: 1,622mg

Fiber: 3g
Carbohydrates: 51g
Sugar: 9g

SPAGHETTI BOLOGNESE

SERVES 1 | PREP: 10 MINUTES | COOK: 20 MINUTES

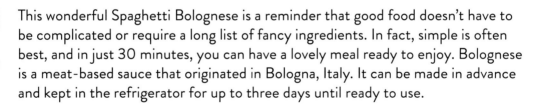 This wonderful Spaghetti Bolognese is a reminder that good food doesn't have to be complicated or require a long list of fancy ingredients. In fact, simple is often best, and in just 30 minutes, you can have a lovely meal ready to enjoy. Bolognese is a meat-based sauce that originated in Bologna, Italy. It can be made in advance and kept in the refrigerator for up to three days until ready to use.

INGREDIENTS

1 tablespoon olive oil

½ cup peeled and chopped yellow onion

1 clove garlic, peeled and minced

1 small carrot, peeled and coarsely chopped

2 ounces ground beef

2 ounces ground Italian sausage

1 (14-ounce) can diced tomatoes, including juice

1 teaspoon dried basil

¼ teaspoon kosher salt

⅛ teaspoon freshly ground black pepper

2 ounces spaghetti noodles, cooked according to package instructions

1. In a 10" skillet over medium heat, heat oil 30 seconds. Add onions, garlic, and carrots and cook until onions become very soft and carrots are tender, about 5 minutes.

2. Add ground beef and ground sausage. Cook, stirring occasionally and breaking up any large lumps, until meat is no longer pink, about 8 minutes.

3. Add tomatoes, dried basil, salt, and pepper and bring to a boil over high heat. Once boiling, reduce heat to low and simmer until sauce thickens, about 10 minutes.

4. Place spaghetti on a medium plate and top with Bolognese. Enjoy.

PER SERVING

Calories: 746   Fiber: 13g
Fat: 33g   Carbohydrates: 87g
Protein: 32g   Sugar: 25g
Sodium: 1,793mg

LOADED BEEF NACHOS

SERVES 1 | PREP: 5 MINUTES | COOK: 15 MINUTES

 These nachos are ideal for movie night, game day, or even as a midweek dinner. Warm tortilla chips are topped with sautéed onions, garlic, ground beef, and cheese. Feel free to add any other favorite toppings you like, such as sour cream, chopped lettuce, and black beans.

INGREDIENTS

2 cups tortilla chips

½ tablespoon olive oil

2 tablespoons peeled and chopped yellow onion

1 clove garlic, peeled and minced

4 ounces ground beef

⅛ teaspoon kosher salt

⅛ teaspoon freshly ground black pepper

⅔ cup shredded Cheddar cheese

1 small vine-ripe tomato, chopped

1 tablespoon chopped jalapeños

1. Preheat oven to 400°F.

2. Line a large baking sheet with foil; spray with cooking spray. Spread chips evenly on pan. Set aside.

3. In a 10" skillet over medium heat, heat oil 30 seconds. Add onions and cook, stirring occasionally, 2 minutes. Add garlic and cook, stirring occasionally, another 1 minute.

4. Add ground beef, salt, and pepper and cook, stirring occasionally, until beef is brown, about 8 minutes. Transfer beef to a large paper towel–lined plate to drain.

5. Scatter drained beef over tortilla chips. Top with remaining toppings.

6. Place pan in oven and bake until cheese melts, about 5 minutes. Enjoy hot.

PER SERVING

Calories: 937
Fat: 62g
Protein: 44g
Sodium: 1,050mg

Fiber: 5g
Carbohydrates: 50g
Sugar: 5g

SHEPHERD'S PIE

SERVES 1 | PREP: 15 MINUTES | COOK: 50 MINUTES

 Shepherd's Pie is a comforting casserole made with ground beef and vegetables, topped with creamy mashed potatoes. Consider adding shredded cheese as a topping during the last 5 minutes of baking for an extra creamy touch.

INGREDIENTS

For Mashed Potatoes

1 medium Yukon Gold potato (about 7 ounces), scrubbed and quartered

¼ cup 1% milk

¼ cup heavy cream

1 clove garlic, peeled and minced

1 tablespoon cold butter

⅛ teaspoon kosher salt

For Stew

½ tablespoon olive oil

2 tablespoons peeled and chopped yellow onion

1 clove garlic, peeled and minced

4 ounces ground beef

⅛ teaspoon kosher salt

1 teaspoon Worcestershire sauce

¼ cup frozen mixed vegetables

¼ cup beef broth

PER SERVING

Calories: 825
Fat: 58g
Protein: 31g
Sodium: 1,137mg
Fiber: 7g
Carbohydrates: 47g
Sugar: 10g

1. **To make Mashed Potatoes:** Place potatoes in a 1-quart saucepan over medium-high heat. Add milk, cream, and garlic and stir. Add extra milk if potatoes are not almost completely covered by liquid. Cook 15 minutes until potatoes are tender.

2. Strain potatoes over a medium bowl and reserve cream mixture.

3. Return potatoes to pan and add ¼ cup cream mixture. Mash potatoes and add additional liquid as needed until thick and creamy.

4. Stir in butter and ⅛ teaspoon salt and set aside.

1. **To make Stew:** In a 10" skillet over medium-high heat, heat oil 30 seconds. Add onions and cook, stirring occasionally, 2 minutes.

2. Add garlic and ground beef and season with salt. Cook, stirring occasionally, until beef is no longer pink, about 4 minutes. Stir in Worcestershire sauce and vegetables.

3. Add broth and bring to a boil over high heat. Once boiling, reduce heat to medium-low and simmer 10 minutes until most of liquid has evaporated. Set aside.

4. Preheat oven to 350°F. Grease an 8-ounce ramekin with butter.

5. Add beef mixture to ramekin and top with mashed potatoes. Bake 20 minutes.

6. Remove ramekin from oven and serve immediately.

ZUCCHINI LASAGNA

SERVES 1 | PREP: 10 MINUTES | COOK: 40 MINUTES

 This small-batch Zucchini Lasagna is made with the wonderful ingredients found in a traditional lasagna—without the high-carb, gluten-filled noodles. The size of your baking dish will determine how many layers you are able to fit. If you use a 5" × 5" baking dish as the recipe calls for, you will get one layer of filling between the noodles. You can use an 8½" x 4½" pan if you want an additional layer.

INGREDIENTS

½ tablespoon olive oil

½ cup peeled and chopped yellow onion

1 clove garlic, peeled and minced

8 ounces ground beef

½ teaspoon Italian seasoning

½ teaspoon kosher salt, divided

⅛ teaspoon freshly ground black pepper

¾ cup tomato sauce, divided

¾ cup ricotta cheese

3 tablespoons Parmesan cheese, divided

1 small zucchini, thinly sliced lengthwise, dried

¾ cup shredded mozzarella cheese, divided

1. Preheat oven to 350°F.

2. In a medium skillet over medium heat, heat oil 30 seconds. Add onions and cook 2 minutes, stirring occasionally.

3. Add minced garlic and cook, stirring occasionally, an additional 1 minute.

4. Add ground beef and sprinkle with Italian seasoning, ¼ teaspoon salt, and pepper. Cook and stir until meat is no longer pink, about 5 minutes.

5. Stir in ½ cup tomato sauce and remaining salt, reduce heat to low, and simmer 3 minutes.

6. While mixture simmers, stir together ricotta and 2 tablespoons Parmesan cheese in a small bowl. Set aside.

7. To assemble lasagna, spread 3 tablespoons meat sauce into bottom of a 5" × 5" baking dish lightly greased with butter or oil. Line bottom of dish with zucchini noodles.

8. Top zucchini with ½ meat sauce, followed by ½ ricotta mixture, and ¼ cup mozzarella.

9. Repeat by adding a second layer of zucchini slices, meat sauce, ricotta mixture, and ¼ cup mozzarella.

Continued on next page

PER SERVING

Calories: 1,288   Fiber: 6g
Fat: 89g   Carbohydrates: 30g
Protein: 92g   Sugar: 14g
Sodium: 2,553mg

10. If you have more room in the dish, top with a final layer zucchini noodles, remaining ¼ cup of tomato sauce, and remaining cheeses. If you don't have room for zucchini, top with remaining sauce and cheeses.

11. Place in the oven and bake 30 minutes until cheese on top has melted.

12. Remove from oven, slice, and enjoy.

How to Dry Out Zucchini Noodles

Lay the noodles on a long cutting board or a tray and lightly sprinkle salt over them. Zucchini contains a lot of water, and the salt pulls this water out of the vegetable noodles while lightly seasoning them at the same time. Once salted, let the zucchini strips sit undisturbed for about 10 minutes, then pat dry with a paper towel.

CHAPTER SIX

FISH AND SEAFOOD MAIN DISHES

Growing up in New Orleans, seafood was an integral part of the meals my family enjoyed every week. But you don't have to live in Louisiana to enjoy seafood—nor should you. Seafood is a versatile protein that can include anything from whitefish to shrimp and crab. Seafood dishes are typically lighter than red meat recipes, and can be very quick and easy to make. The great flavors that naturally come from seafood can also be enhanced with something as simple as lemon juice, or you can spice things up with a variety of seasonings.

In this chapter, you'll find my favorite seafood meals for one, including a number of recipes from my time spent in New Orleans. So take a quick trip down South with the Shrimp Creole, Shrimp and Sausage Jambalaya, or Crawfish Beignets! On the lighter side, you'll also discover Baked Catfish, Lemon Garlic Baked Shrimp, and Fish Tacos with Curried Broccoli Slaw. Filling, easy to make, healthy, and without any of the waste of multiple-serving recipes, these dishes are sure to please. So dive in!

BAKED STUFFED FISH FILLET

SERVES 1 | PREP: 10 MINUTES | COOK: 30 MINUTES

 A delectable fish fillet stuffed with sautéed bacon, celery, onions, and garlic, this savory meal is the perfect amount for anyone cooking for one. Although the recipe calls for using catfish, feel free to use flounder or snapper if you prefer. Enjoy with pasta or rice, or enjoy on its own.

INGREDIENTS

1 (8-ounce) catfish fillet

⅛ teaspoon kosher salt

⅛ teaspoon freshly ground black pepper

1 teaspoon olive oil

1 slice bacon, chopped

2 tablespoons chopped celery

2 tablespoons peeled and chopped yellow onion

1 clove garlic, peeled and minced

1 teaspoon finely chopped fresh parsley

½ tablespoon butter, melted, divided

2 tablespoons dry white wine

2 tablespoons grated Parmesan cheese

⅛ teaspoon smoked paprika

1. Preheat oven to 350°F.

2. Sprinkle fish fillet with salt and pepper. Set aside.

3. In a 10" skillet over medium-high heat, heat oil 30 seconds. Add bacon, celery, and onions and sauté until bacon is crisp and vegetables are soft, about 3 minutes. Add garlic and cook an additional 2 minutes.

4. Remove skillet from heat and stir in parsley.

5. Spread mixture over fish, roll fish up, and fasten with a toothpick.

6. Add 1 teaspoon melted butter to a 5" × 5" baking dish and swirl to coat bottom of dish. Place fish in dish.

7. Pour remaining butter over fish, and add wine. Sprinkle with Parmesan cheese and paprika.

8. Place dish in oven and bake 30 minutes.

9. Transfer to a medium plate and serve hot.

What Are the Best Non-Alcoholic Substitutes for Wine?

If you're cooking and realize that you don't have any wine on hand, or want to leave the alcohol out altogether, don't dismiss the recipe just yet: It's easy to make substitutions. Use chicken or vegetable broth, red or white wine vinegar, or lemon juice instead of the alcohol.

PER SERVING

Calories: 484
Fat: 30g
Protein: 44g
Sodium: 825mg

Fiber: 1g
Carbohydrates: 4g
Sugar: 1g

SHRIMP CREOLE

SERVES 1 | PREP: 15 MINUTES | COOK: 35 MINUTES

 Shrimp Creole is a classic Louisiana dish made with garlic, onions, bell peppers, and tomatoes. Based on my family's traditional recipe, this single-serving version may become a favorite of yours too! Enjoy with rice.

INGREDIENTS

1 tablespoon butter

½ cup peeled and chopped yellow onion

¼ cup chopped and seeded green bell peppers

1 medium stalk celery, chopped

2 cloves garlic, peeled and minced

¼ teaspoon kosher salt

⅛ teaspoon cayenne pepper

1 (14.5-ounce) can diced tomatoes including juice

¼ cup water

½ tablespoon all-purpose flour

¼ teaspoon Worcestershire sauce

¼ teaspoon hot sauce

½ cup peeled, deveined shrimp (about 10 medium)

½ teaspoon Creole seasoning

1. In a 10" saucepan or skillet over medium heat, melt butter 30 seconds. Add onions, peppers, celery and garlic to pan. Season with salt and cayenne pepper and cook, stirring occasionally, until slightly softened, about 7 minutes.

2. Stir in diced tomatoes. Bring mixture to a boil over high heat, then reduce heat to low and simmer 10 minutes.

3. In a small bowl, whisk together water and flour. Add to tomato mixture and continue simmering 5 minutes, stirring occasionally.

4. Add Worcestershire sauce and hot sauce and continue simmering 5 minutes.

5. Season shrimp with Creole seasoning and add to pan. Cook shrimp until pink and cooked through, about 6 minutes.

6. Top mixture with chopped green onions, then transfer to a medium plate and enjoy.

Stovetop Single-Serving Rice
To make a single serving of white rice on the stove, bring ½ cup water, ¼ teaspoon kosher salt, and ½ tablespoon butter to a boil over high heat in a small saucepan. Stir in ¼ cup rice, then reduce heat to a simmer on low heat and cover. Simmer for 20 minutes until all water is absorbed.

PER SERVING

Calories: 351	*Fiber: 11g*
Fat: 14g	*Carbohydrates: 47g*
Protein: 17g	*Sugar: 24g*
Sodium: 1,746mg	

SHRIMP AND SAUSAGE JAMBALAYA

SERVES 1 | PREP: 10 MINUTES | COOK: 25 MINUTES

Jambalaya is a dish consisting mainly of meat and vegetables cooked with rice. It is similar to gumbo, with the main difference being that the rice is cooked along with the rest of the ingredients, while in a gumbo, the rice is cooked separately. In the case of this single-serving jambalaya, sausage and shrimp are cooked along with the "holy trinity" of vegetables: onions, celery, and green peppers.

INGREDIENTS

½ tablespoon olive oil

2 tablespoons peeled and chopped yellow onion

2 tablespoons chopped celery

1 clove garlic, peeled and minced

¼ cup chopped and seeded green bell peppers

¼ teaspoon kosher salt

⅛ teaspoon cayenne pepper

¼ pound smoked sausage, cut into half moons

¼ pound shrimp, peeled and deveined

½ cup canned diced tomatoes, drained

½ cup long-grain white rice

1½ cups chicken broth

1. In a 10" skillet over medium heat, heat oil 30 seconds. Add onions, celery, garlic, and green peppers. Season with salt and cayenne pepper, and cook, stirring constantly, until vegetables have softened, about 5 minutes.

2. Add sausage and cook, still stirring, 2 minutes. Add shrimp and cook, constantly stirring, 2 minutes until shrimp are almost completely pink.

3. Stir in tomatoes and rice and cook, stirring constantly, 1 minute, then add broth.

4. Bring to a boil over high heat, then reduce heat to medium-low, cover, and cook until rice is tender and most of liquid is absorbed, about 25 minutes.

5. Spoon into a medium bowl and enjoy hot.

Do You Need to Remove the Vein in Shrimp?

The "vein" in a shrimp is not truly a vein: It is actually a part of the digestive tract. Sometimes the vein is very prominent, and other times you will barely notice it. The vein isn't really harmful if you eat it; however, it can add a gritty texture. To remove the vein, make a shallow cut with a sharp knife along the back of the shrimp and gently pull the vein out with the tip of the knife.

PER SERVING

Calories: 783   Fiber: 4g
Fat: 24g   Carbohydrates: 92g
Protein: 47g   Sugar: 7g
Sodium: 3,475mg

SALMON BAKED IN FOIL

SERVES 1 | PREP: 10 MINUTES | COOK: 20 MINUTES

 This recipe features a salmon fillet baked in foil, allowing for a flavorful meal with little cleanup. Specifically, baking salmon in foil traps the moisture inside to prevent the salmon from drying out. The fillet is topped with butter, spices, and lemon and bakes in just minutes.

INGREDIENTS

1 (6-ounce) salmon fillet

1 tablespoon butter, softened

¼ teaspoon garlic powder

¼ teaspoon dried tarragon

⅛ teaspoon red pepper flakes

⅛ teaspoon kosher salt

1 slice lemon

1. Preheat oven to 400°F.

2. Place salmon in center of a large piece of aluminum foil. Set aside.

3. Place the softened butter in a small bowl and add garlic powder, tarragon, red pepper flakes, and salt. Stir to blend.

4. Spoon butter mixture over salmon and spread to cover entire fillet. Top with lemon slice.

5. Cover fillet with another sheet of aluminum foil and pinch edges together to seal tightly. Place salmon foil packet on an ungreased baking sheet.

6. Place baking sheet in oven and bake 25 minutes until salmon is cooked through and flakes easily with a fork.

7. Transfer to a medium plate, unwrap from foil, and enjoy.

PER SERVING

Calories: 458   Fiber: 0g
Fat: 34g   Carbohydrates: 1g
Protein: 35g   Sugar: 0g
Sodium: 393mg

CAJUN SHRIMP AND VEGETABLE FOIL PACK

SERVES 1 | PREP: 10 MINUTES | COOK: 10 MINUTES

 This perfectly portioned foil pack is virtually mess-free! All of the ingredients bake right in the pack, making this an easy meal to whip up with very little cleanup. Although this recipe uses an oven, you can also cook it on a grill.

INGREDIENTS

½ medium summer squash, diced

½ small red pepper, seeded and chopped

2 slices peeled medium yellow onion

4 ounces medium shrimp, peeled and deveined

¼ teaspoon Creole seasoning

¼ teaspoon lemon juice

1. Preheat oven to 375°F.

2. Place all ingredients on a large piece of aluminum foil, then fold up and press sides together to create a packet.

3. Place packet on a rack in the oven and bake 10 minutes.

4. Remove packet from oven, open, and enjoy while hot.

Easy Creole Seasoning

You can find Creole seasoning in the spice aisle at your local grocery store, but you can also make your own at home by blending together 2½ tablespoons paprika, 2 tablespoons kosher salt, 2 tablespoons garlic powder, 1 tablespoon freshly ground black pepper, 1 tablespoon onion powder, 1 tablespoon cayenne pepper, 1 tablespoon dried oregano, and 1 tablespoon dried thyme. Keep it in an airtight container in your pantry, and enjoy sprinkled over chicken, fish, and pasta.

PER SERVING

Calories: 139
Fat: 2g
Protein: 18g
Sodium: 654mg

Fiber: 3g
Carbohydrates: 13g
Sugar: 7g

ROASTED SALMON WITH MAPLE AND MUSTARD

 SERVES 1 | PREP: 5 MINUTES | COOK: 15 MINUTES

This is an incredibly easy and tasty salmon recipe that can be ready in 30 minutes! Pair with asparagus, potatoes, or whatever side you choose.

INGREDIENTS

½ teaspoon Dijon mustard

1½ teaspoons pure maple syrup

1 (5-ounce) salmon fillet

⅛ teaspoon kosher salt

⅛ teaspoon freshly ground black pepper

1. Preheat oven to 400°F.

2. Whisk together Dijon mustard and maple syrup in a small bowl. Set aside.

3. Place salmon fillet on a baking sheet lightly greased with oil. Sprinkle top of fillet with salt and pepper, then pour mustard sauce over top.

4. Bake until just cooked through, about 13 minutes. Enjoy immediately.

PER SERVING

Calories: 324
Fat: 19g
Protein: 29g
Sodium: 436mg

Fiber: 0g
Carbohydrates: 7g
Sugar: 6g

BAKED FISH WITH SALSA

SERVES 1 | PREP: 5 MINUTES | COOK: 20 MINUTES

 It's hard to believe how quickly and easily this baked fish comes together. One lean and firm fish fillet is topped with salsa, baked for 20 minutes, and topped with melted cheese; it's the perfect meal for a busy evening. You can use catfish or haddock instead of cod if preferred.

INGREDIENTS

½ tablespoon olive oil

1 (6-ounce) cod fillet

¼ cup mild salsa

2 tablespoons shredded Monterey jack cheese

1. Preheat oven to 400°F.
2. Grease a 5" × 5" baking dish with olive oil. Place fish fillet in dish and spoon salsa over fillet.
3. Place dish in oven and bake 20 minutes.
4. Remove fish from oven and top with shredded cheese. Return to oven and bake an additional 2 minutes until cheese is melted.
5. Transfer fish to a medium plate and enjoy.

PER SERVING

Calories: 270

Fat: 12g

Protein: 35g

Sodium: 632mg

Fiber: 1g

Carbohydrates: 4g

Sugar: 3g

SHRIMP FETTUCCINE

SERVES 1 | PREP: 5 MINUTES | COOK: 20 MINUTES

 This wonderful Shrimp Fettuccine is a flavorful, easy meal that cooks quickly. Healthy, hearty and the perfect amount for anyone cooking for one, it just may become a staple. The recipe calls for ¼ teaspoon of red pepper flakes, but if you want your shrimp on the milder side, use less.

INGREDIENTS

1 tablespoon cold butter

2 cloves garlic, peeled and minced

¼ teaspoon crushed red pepper flakes

2 ounces shrimp, peeled and deveined

⅛ teaspoon kosher salt

4 ounces uncooked fettuccine noodles, cooked according to package instructions

½ tablespoon olive oil

1 tablespoon grated Parmesan cheese

1. In a 10" skillet over medium heat, melt butter 30 seconds. Add garlic and red pepper and cook, stirring occasionally, 1 minute.

2. Add shrimp and cook, stirring occasionally, until shrimp is cooked through and pink, about 3 minutes.

3. Stir in salt, then remove skillet from heat.

4. Add fettuccine to skillet and top with olive oil. Toss to combine.

5. Transfer Shrimp Fettuccine to a medium plate and top with Parmesan cheese. Enjoy.

Cooking for One with Shrimp
When cooking for one, keeping your freezer stocked with a few bags of frozen shrimp will make it easy to whip up a wonderful, seemingly fancy meal in just minutes. You'll thank yourself at the end of those extra-long days.

PER SERVING

Calories: 667   Fiber: 5g
Fat: 23g   Carbohydrates: 88g
Protein: 26g   Sugar: 2g
Sodium: 1,062mg

LEMON GARLIC BAKED SHRIMP

SERVES 1 | PREP: 15 MINUTES | COOK: 10 MINUTES

 Shrimp, butter, a handful of spices, and lemon juice are all you need for this great one-pan meal. The shrimp cooks quickly in the oven and is delightful served with rice, pasta, or a side of your favorite steamed vegetables.

INGREDIENTS

1 tablespoon butter, melted

¼ teaspoon lemon juice

⅛ teaspoon kosher salt

⅛ teaspoon dried tarragon

⅛ teaspoon garlic powder

⅛ teaspoon freshly ground black pepper

4 ounces medium shrimp, peeled and deveined

1. Preheat oven to 400°F.
2. In a small bowl, whisk together butter, lemon juice, salt, tarragon, garlic powder, and pepper.
3. Place shrimp in a single layer in an ungreased 5" × 5" baking dish and stir in butter mixture.
4. Place dish in oven and bake until shrimp is pink, firm, and cooked through, about 8 minutes.
5. Transfer to a medium plate and enjoy immediately.

PER SERVING

Calories: 184
Fat: 13g
Protein: 16g
Sodium: 937mg

Fiber: 0g
Carbohydrates: 1g
Sugar: 0g

SHRIMP AND PROSCIUTTO PASTA

SERVES 1 | PREP: 10 MINUTES | COOK: 20 MINUTES

 This creamy and delicious meal is filled with plump shrimp and salty prosciutto, all simmering in a wonderfully rich sauce. The recipe calls for using white wine, but you can easily substitute with chicken broth.

INGREDIENTS

½ tablespoon olive oil

1 clove garlic, peeled and minced

¼ cup chopped prosciutto

½ cup (about 10 medium) peeled, deveined shrimp

¼ cup dry white wine

¼ cup heavy cream

¼ cup shredded Parmesan cheese

1½ cups bowtie pasta, cooked according to package instructions

9 cherry tomatoes, chopped

1. In a 10" skillet over medium heat, heat oil 30 seconds. Add garlic, prosciutto, and shrimp and cook 4 minutes until shrimp are pink.

2. Add wine and cook, stirring occasionally, 1 minute.

3. Stir in cream and cheese and cook, stirring frequently, until the cheese is melted, about 30 seconds.

4. Gently fold in cooked pasta and garnish with tomatoes.

5. Transfer to a medium plate and enjoy immediately.

PER SERVING

Calories: 794
Fat: 38g
Protein: 38g
Sodium: 1,354mg

Fiber: 6g
Carbohydrates: 74g
Sugar: 7g

SMOKY BAKED CATFISH

SERVES 1 | PREP: 10 MINUTES | COOK: 20 MINUTES

 There aren't many meals that are easier to prepare than this Smoky Baked Catfish recipe. Smoked paprika is the key to the incredible flavor. Enjoy with rice or buttered noodles.

INGREDIENTS

½ teaspoon smoked paprika

½ teaspoon Italian seasoning

⅛ teaspoon onion powder

⅛ teaspoon kosher salt

⅛ teaspoon freshly ground black pepper

1 (6-ounce) catfish fillet

1 tablespoon butter, melted

1. Preheat oven to 350°F. Grease a 5" × 5" baking dish with butter or oil.

2. Combine smoked paprika, Italian seasoning, onion powder, salt, and pepper in a small bowl. Sprinkle over both sides of fillet.

3. Place fillet in baking dish, top with butter, and bake 20 minutes until fish flakes easily with a fork.

4. Transfer fillet to a medium plate and enjoy.

PER SERVING

Calories: 329

Fat: 23g

Protein: 29g

Sodium: 476mg

Fiber: 1g

Carbohydrates: 1g

Sugar: 0g

EGGS WITH SMOKED SALMON AND PESTO

SERVES 1 | PREP: 10 MINUTES | COOK: 10 MINUTES

 Eggs aren't just for breakfast, as in this recipe. Eggs are piled high on top of smoked salmon and a thick piece of bread for a satisfying lunch or dinner. French bread is a favorite to use in this dish, but other great options include whole wheat, sourdough, and pumpernickel.

INGREDIENTS

½ tablespoon cold butter

2 large eggs, lightly beaten

⅛ teaspoon kosher salt

⅛ teaspoon freshly ground black pepper

1 tablespoon minced fresh chives

1 medium slice French bread, toasted

1 tablespoon pesto

2 ounces thinly sliced smoked salmon

1. In a small skillet over medium-low heat, melt butter 30 seconds. Add eggs and season with salt and pepper.

2. Add chives and cook, stirring with a rubber or silicone spatula, until big lumps of eggs begin to form, about 1 minute. Continue cooking by folding eggs until thickened and no liquid remains, about 3 minutes more. Remove skillet from heat.

3. Place toast on a medium plate and spread pesto over one side. Place slices of smoked salmon over pesto.

4. Spoon eggs over smoked salmon and enjoy immediately.

PER SERVING

Calories: 490   Fiber: 2g
Fat: 26g   Carbohydrates: 33g
Protein: 30g   Sugar: 3g
Sodium: 1,328mg

BROILED SALMON WITH ROASTED ZUCCHINI

SERVES 1 | PREP: 5 MINUTES | COOK: 10 MINUTES

Quick, delicious, *and* healthy, this single-serving Broiled Salmon with Roasted Zucchini recipe can be made in under 10 minutes. For a heartier meal, pair with potatoes.

INGREDIENTS

1 (4-ounce) salmon fillet, patted dry

1 medium zucchini, ends removed, diced

2 tablespoons olive oil, divided

½ teaspoon kosher salt, divided

¼ teaspoon freshly ground black pepper, divided

½ medium lemon

1. Preheat broiler to low.

2. Place salmon fillet on one side of an ungreased baking sheet. Set aside.

3. Place zucchini into a medium bowl and toss with 1 tablespoon oil, ¼ teaspoon salt, and ⅛ teaspoon pepper. Pour mixture on opposite side of baking sheet.

4. Pour remaining oil over salmon and sprinkle with remaining salt and pepper. Rub oil, salt, and pepper into salmon and ensure oil is also on bottom of salmon.

5. Place sheet in oven and cook 8 minutes.

6. Remove sheet from oven and squeeze lemon over top of both salmon and zucchini before serving.

PER SERVING

Calories: 515
Fat: 43g
Protein: 26g
Sodium: 1,246mg

Fiber: 2g
Carbohydrates: 8g
Sugar: 5g

TUNA CASSEROLE

SERVES 1 | PREP: 15 MINUTES | COOK: 20 MINUTES

 This small-batch Tuna Casserole has come a long way from the tuna casseroles of my childhood. Made with a rich homemade sauce, it has enhanced creamy flavors and a crisp and buttery topping. Enjoy on its own, or portioned as a side.

INGREDIENTS

1 tablespoon cold butter

¼ cup peeled and chopped yellow onion

1 tablespoon all-purpose flour

½ teaspoon kosher salt

¼ teaspoon freshly ground black pepper

¼ teaspoon ground nutmeg

¼ teaspoon dried thyme

⅛ teaspoon garlic powder

½ cup 1% milk

¼ cup heavy cream

1 teaspoon lemon juice

½ cup shredded Cheddar cheese

¼ cup grated Parmesan cheese

1 (5-ounce) can tuna, drained

½ cup elbow macaroni, cooked according to package instructions

1½ tablespoons seasoned bread crumbs

1 tablespoon butter, melted

PER SERVING

Calories: 1,338   *Fiber: 4g*
Fat: 83g   *Carbohydrates: 74g*
Protein: 74g   *Sugar: 11g*
Sodium: 2,727mg

1. Preheat oven to 350°F.

2. Grease an oven-safe 8-ounce ramekin or 5" × 5" baking dish with nonstick cooking spray. Set aside.

3. In a small saucepan over medium heat, melt butter 30 seconds. Add onions and stir until softened, about 4 minutes.

4. Stir in flour, salt, pepper, nutmeg, thyme, and garlic powder and cook, stirring constantly, 1 minute.

5. Whisk in milk, cream, and lemon juice and let simmer, whisking occasionally, until thickened, about 5 minutes.

6. Remove from heat and stir in cheeses.

7. In a medium bowl, combine tuna with sauce and pasta. Pour into prepared baking dish.

8. In a small bowl, mix together bread crumbs and melted butter. Sprinkle over top of casserole.

9. Place dish in oven and bake 22 minutes until topping is golden. Enjoy hot.

Consider Canned Fish

Canned fish such as tuna, salmon, and sardines are excellent budget-friendly options. Canned fish can be nutritious, low in sodium, and rich in omega-3s—just read the labels before purchasing for the best selections. Keep cans stocked in your pantry for quick salads and sandwiches for one.

LEMON AND HERB–ROASTED SALMON

SERVES 1 | PREP: 5 MINUTES | COOK: 15 MINUTES

 This simple roasted salmon is flavored perfectly with a delightful blend of spices and lemon juice. The fish cooks quickly and is a light, healthy, and absolutely delicious meal. Pair with your favorite cooked vegetable or a side salad.

INGREDIENTS

1 (5-ounce) salmon fillet

½ tablespoon olive oil

½ tablespoon softened butter

⅛ teaspoon kosher salt

⅛ teaspoon freshly ground black pepper

⅛ teaspoon dried rosemary

⅛ teaspoon garlic powder

2 slices lemon

1. Preheat oven to 375°F. Line a baking sheet with aluminum foil lightly greased with cooking spray.

2. Place salmon on foil and drizzle oil over top. Set aside.

3. Place butter in a small bowl and add salt, pepper, rosemary, and garlic powder. Stir to blend.

4. Spoon butter mixture over salmon and spread to cover. Top with lemon slices and cover with another sheet of aluminum foil. Pinch the edges of the foil together to seal tightly.

5. Place sheet in oven and bake 16 minutes until salmon is cooked through. Enjoy hot.

PER SERVING

Calories: 408   Fiber: 0g
Fat: 32g   Carbohydrates: 1g
Protein: 29g   Sugar: 0g
Sodium: 376mg

SHRIMP QUESADILLA

SERVES 1 | **PREP: 15 MINUTES** | **COOK: 10 MINUTES**

 This healthy quesadilla takes just minutes to cook! Shrimp is marinated in lemon juice, chili powder, and salt and cooks quickly on the stove. Enjoy with a dollop of sour cream.

INGREDIENTS

¼ pound medium shrimp, peeled and deveined

⅛ teaspoon chili powder

⅛ teaspoon kosher salt

1 tablespoon lemon juice

1 tablespoon room temperature butter

½ tablespoon olive oil

2 (8") flour tortillas

½ cup shredded Monterey jack cheese

1 tablespoon peeled and chopped yellow onion

¼ medium avocado, pitted, peeled, and sliced

1 tablespoon chopped fresh cilantro

1. Toss shrimp in a small bowl with chili powder, salt, and lemon juice. Let sit 10 minutes, then drain and set aside.

2. In a 10" skillet over medium-high heat, melt butter 30 seconds. Add shrimp and cook 1 minute on each side, until pink. Transfer shrimp to a large plate and slice in half. Set aside.

3. Add oil to skillet and lower heat to medium. Place one tortilla in skillet and cook 2 minutes on each side.

4. Place shrimp on tortilla and top with cheese and onions. Place second tortilla on top. Flip and cook until cheese melts, about 3 minutes.

5. Remove quesadilla from pan and cut into 6 triangles. Enjoy with avocado slices and cilantro.

PER SERVING

Calories: 860
Fat: 51g
Protein: 39g
Sodium: 1,756mg
Fiber: 7g
Carbohydrates: 62g
Sugar: 1g

SALMON AND ASPARAGUS SHEET PAN DINNER

SERVES 1 | PREP: 10 MINUTES | COOK: 15 MINUTES

 Salmon and Asparagus Sheet Pan Dinner: a one-pan meal that makes cleanup easy! Depending on the size of your asparagus, they might need a little more time to cook. If that's the case, transfer the salmon to a plate and cover with foil, then return the baking sheet to the oven to finish cooking. If you really love asparagus, feel free to add in more spears!

INGREDIENTS

1 tablespoon butter, softened

1 teaspoon olive oil, divided

¼ teaspoon dried basil

¼ teaspoon kosher salt, divided

⅛ teaspoon freshly ground black pepper

6 asparagus spears, woody ends removed, rinsed

1 (4-ounce) salmon fillet

1 tablespoon lemon juice

1. Preheat oven to 425°F.

2. In a small bowl, stir together butter, ½ teaspoon oil, basil, ⅛ teaspoon salt, and pepper. Set aside.

3. On one side of a rimmed baking sheet, toss asparagus with ½ teaspoon oil and ⅛ teaspoon salt. Spread asparagus in one layer across side of baking sheet.

4. Grease other side of baking sheet with oil, then place salmon fillet skin-side down on sheet. Spoon butter mixture over top of salmon.

5. Place baking sheet in oven and bake until asparagus are tender and salmon is cooked, about 15 minutes.

6. Transfer asparagus to a medium plate and top with salmon. Drizzle lemon juice over the top. Enjoy.

PER SERVING

Calories: 313
Fat: 21g
Protein: 26g
Sodium: 672mg

Fiber: 2g
Carbohydrates: 5g
Sugar: 2g

BARBECUE SHRIMP

SERVES 1 | PREP: 10 MINUTES | COOK: 10 MINUTES

 This Barbecue Shrimp is buttery, perfectly spiced, and incredibly delicious. Ready in minutes, it can be enjoyed on its own or served with cooked rice for a hearty meal.

INGREDIENTS

1 tablespoon room temperature butter

1 clove garlic, peeled and thinly sliced

1 tablespoon Worcestershire sauce

4 ounces shrimp, peeled and deveined

¼ teaspoon Creole seasoning

1. In a 10" skillet over medium-high heat, melt butter 30 seconds.

2. Reduce heat to low and add garlic, Worcestershire sauce, shrimp, and seasoning. Cook 3 minutes on each side until all shrimp are pink.

3. Transfer shrimp to a medium bowl and enjoy hot.

PER SERVING

Calories: 200
Fat: 13g
Protein: 16g
Sodium: 811mg

Fiber: 0g
Carbohydrates: 5g
Sugar: 2g

CRAWFISH PASTA

SERVES 1 | PREP: 10 MINUTES | COOK: 25 MINUTES

 This New Orleans–inspired Crawfish Pasta is so easy to make and filled with the "holy trinity" of vegetables (green peppers, onions, and celery) and plenty of crawfish. Cooked in under 30 minutes, this creamy dish is perfectly spiced and incredibly delicious!

INGREDIENTS

1½ tablespoons room temperature butter, divided

2 tablespoons peeled and chopped yellow onion

2 tablespoons chopped and seeded green bell peppers

2 tablespoons chopped celery

1 clove garlic, peeled and minced

1 tablespoon all-purpose flour

½ teaspoon tomato paste

1.5 ounces (about ½ cup) cooked crawfish tails

¼ teaspoon Creole seasoning

¾ cup low-sodium chicken broth

2 ounces (about ½ cup) fettuccini pasta, cooked according to package instructions

1. In a 10" skillet over medium heat, melt 1 tablespoon butter 30 seconds. Add onions, bell peppers, and celery. Cook until vegetables are soft, about 3 minutes.

2. Add garlic and cook 2 minutes, then add flour and cook, stirring constantly, another 1 minute.

3. Stir in tomato paste and cook, stirring constantly, 1 minute. Add crawfish and Creole seasoning and cook 3 additional minutes.

4. Pour in broth and bring to a boil over high heat. Once boiling, reduce heat to low and simmer, stirring frequently, until mixture thickens, about 3 minutes.

5. Stir in pasta and remaining butter, then transfer to a medium plate and enjoy.

What Is the Holy Trinity of Vegetables?

If you're from Louisiana, you already know that the holy trinity of vegetables is the base of New Orleans cooking. In fact, almost every traditional New Orleans recipe consists of these three aromatic vegetables: onions, green bell peppers, and celery.

PER SERVING

Calories: 484
Fat: 20g
Protein: 21g
Sodium: 291mg

Fiber: 4g
Carbohydrates: 55g
Sugar: 3g

MEDITERRANEAN SHRIMP AND PASTA

SERVES 1 | PREP: 10 MINUTES | COOK: 35 MINUTES

 This Mediterranean pasta dish is loaded with shrimp, roasted tomatoes, olives, and feta cheese and is bursting with flavor. It looks gourmet, but is so easy to make, and can be ready in minutes! Put your own spin on it with the addition of peppers, grilled chicken, or a different kind of pasta.

INGREDIENTS

2 medium plum tomatoes, halved lengthwise

3 tablespoons olive oil, divided

1 clove garlic, peeled and chopped

1 teaspoon Italian seasoning

⅛ teaspoon crushed red pepper flakes

⅛ teaspoon kosher salt

⅛ teaspoon freshly ground black pepper

2 ounces penne pasta, cooked according to package instructions

½ tablespoon room temperature butter

4 ounces shrimp, peeled and deveined

¼ cup pitted Kalamata olives

2 tablespoons feta cheese

1. Preheat oven to 400°F.

2. Place tomatoes, cut-side up, on an ungreased, foil-lined baking sheet. Mix 1 tablespoon oil, garlic, Italian seasoning, red pepper flakes, salt, and pepper in a small bowl. Spoon over tomatoes. Drizzle with another 1 tablespoon olive oil.

3. Roast tomatoes in oven 40 minutes, until the to-matoes are soft and browned on top.

4. Place pasta in a medium bowl, stir in remaining oil, and set aside.

5. In a 10" skillet over medium heat, melt butter 30 seconds. Add shrimp, cover, and cook shrimp 3 minutes on one side, then flip and cook an addi-tional 4 minutes.

6. Transfer shrimp to bowl with pasta.

7. Coarsely chop ½ tomatoes and add them, along with remaining tomatoes and their juices to pasta. Toss to mix well.

8. Stir in Kalamata olives and feta. Enjoy immediately.

PER SERVING

Calories: 915
Fat: 66g
Protein: 28g
Sodium: 2,062mg

Fiber: 5g
Carbohydrates: 54g
Sugar: 5g

BAKED COD WITH CHERMOULA

SERVES 1 | PREP: 15 MINUTES | COOK: 30 MINUTES

 This amazing Baked Cod recipe is made with roasted potatoes and topped with an easy-to-make Moroccan chermoula. An added bonus is that everything cooks in one pan for easy cleanup!

INGREDIENTS

½ cup fresh cilantro leaves

½ cup fresh parsley leaves

1 clove garlic, peeled

¼ teaspoon ground cumin

¼ teaspoon sweet paprika

⅛ teaspoon ground coriander

⅛ teaspoon cayenne pepper

¼ teaspoon kosher salt, divided

1 teaspoon lemon juice

¼ cup olive oil

1 (8-ounce) cod fillet

4 small (about 6 ounces) red potatoes, scrubbed and diced

1. Preheat oven to 350°F.

2. Place cilantro leaves, parsley leaves, garlic, spices, ⅛ teaspoon salt, lemon juice, and oil in the base of a food processor. Pulse until smooth.

3. Place cod on a baking sheet lightly greased with butter or oil. Sprinkle with ⅛ teaspoon salt.

4. Scatter diced potatoes around cod. Spoon chermoula over both cod and potatoes.

5. Place baking sheet in oven and bake 30 minutes until cooked through.

6. Remove from oven and transfer to a medium plate. Enjoy.

What Is Chermoula?

Chermoula is much like a pesto. It's made with cilantro and parsley leaves, garlic, olive oil, lemon juice, and a mix of spices. You can either chop the cilantro and parsley by hand or add them to a food processor to finely chop.

PER SERVING

Calories: 783
Fat: 56g
Protein: 40g
Sodium: 757mg

Fiber: 5g
Carbohydrates: 31g
Sugar: 3g

FISH TACOS
WITH CURRIED BROCCOLI SLAW

SERVES 1 | PREP: 10 MINUTES | COOK: 15 MINUTES

 Quick and easy fish tacos are the perfect seafood dish for one. Although the recipe calls for tilapia, feel free to use catfish, red snapper, or rainbow trout instead— whatever your taste buds prefer!

INGREDIENTS

½ tablespoon olive oil

⅛ teaspoon chili powder

⅛ teaspoon curry powder

⅛ teaspoon garlic powder

⅛ teaspoon kosher salt

1 (6-ounce) tilapia fillet

1½ cups broccoli slaw

½ tablespoon lime juice

½ tablespoon white wine vinegar

¼ teaspoon curry powder

1 tablespoon pure honey

⅛ teaspoon kosher salt

⅛ teaspoon freshly ground black pepper

2 (8") flour tortillas

1. Preheat oven to 375°F.

2. Stir together oil, chili powder, curry powder, garlic powder, and salt in a small bowl. Brush mixture on both sides of fish fillet.

3. Place fish on an ungreased, foil-lined baking sheet and bake 14 minutes until fish flakes easily with a fork.

4. Pour broccoli slaw into a medium bowl and set aside.

5. In a small bowl, combine lime juice, white wine vinegar, curry powder, honey, salt, and pepper. Pour over broccoli slaw and toss to coat.

6. Warm tortillas by either placing them one at a time in a microwave on high for 20 seconds, or in a frying pan over medium-high heat 5 minutes, flipping halfway through.

7. To construct tacos, break up cooked fish and divide on warmed tortillas. Top with broccoli slaw. Enjoy.

PER SERVING

Calories: 650
Fat: 17g
Protein: 47g
Sodium: 1,186mg

Fiber: 8g
Carbohydrates: 80g
Sugar: 20g

CRAWFISH BEIGNETS

MAKES 5 BEIGNETS | PREP: 15 MINUTES | COOK: 10 MINUTES

 Beignets are not just for dessert—and these crispy Crawfish Beignets prove it. Enjoy with a spicy remoulade sauce. This New Orleans–inspired small-batch recipe yields five savory, crawfish-filled beignets. It's a Louisiana tradition, ready in minutes!

INGREDIENTS

For Beignets

½ cup all-purpose flour

½ teaspoon baking powder

¼ teaspoon Creole seasoning

¼ teaspoon kosher salt

⅛ teaspoon ground ginger

1 clove garlic, peeled and minced

1 green onion, finely chopped (about 2 tablespoons)

2 tablespoons chopped parsley

¼ cup (about 1 ounce) crawfish tail meat

¼ teaspoon hot sauce

¼ cup water

Canola oil for frying

For Remoulade Sauce

2 tablespoons mayonnaise

1 tablespoon stone-ground mustard

½ teaspoon olive oil

¼ teaspoon horseradish

¼ teaspoon lemon juice

⅛ teaspoon smoked paprika

¼ teaspoon hot sauce

1. **To make Beignets:** Combine flour, baking powder, Creole seasoning, salt, and ginger in a medium bowl.

2. Stir in minced garlic, green onions, parsley, and crawfish tail meat, then add hot sauce and water. Set aside.

3. In a deep, 2-quart saucepan add enough canola oil to come halfway up sides. Heat oil to 350°F over high heat.

4. Using a large metal spoon, carefully drop ⅕ beignet mixture into oil. Repeat with remaining mixture, and fry 4 minutes until golden brown and crispy.

5. Using a slotted spoon, remove beignets from pan and drain on a large paper towel–lined plate 5 minutes.

1. **To make Remoulade Sauce:** In a small bowl, mix together mayonnaise, mustard, oil, horseradish, lemon juice, smoked paprika, and hot sauce. Enjoy on side for dipping.

PER SERVING (1 BEIGNET)

Calories: 132

Fat: 9g

Protein: 2g

Sodium: 268mg

Fiber: 1g

Carbohydrates: 10g

Sugar: 0g

SHRIMP TACOS WITH AVOCADO PURÉE

SERVES 1 | PREP: 10 MINUTES | COOK: 15 MINUTES

 Made with just a few fresh ingredients, these delicious Shrimp Tacos with Avocado Purée can be prepared and on your dinner table in under 30 minutes! If you can get fresh shrimp, great. If not, frozen shrimp works just as well.

INGREDIENTS

For Shrimp

1 cup shrimp, peeled and deveined (about 20 medium)

¼ teaspoon Cajun seasoning

½ tablespoon room temperature butter

2 cloves garlic, peeled and minced

For Avocado Purée

1 medium avocado, halved and pitted

½ cup plain low-fat yogurt

1 tablespoon lime juice

2 cups fresh spinach leaves

3 tablespoons olive oil

½ teaspoon kosher salt

¼ teaspoon ground cumin

¼ teaspoon chili powder

For Tacos

2 (8") flour tortillas

¼ cup fresh cilantro, chopped

1. **To make Shrimp:** Place shrimp in a medium bowl. Add seasoning and toss to coat. Let stand 5 minutes.

2. In a 10" skillet over medium-high heat, melt butter 30 seconds. Add garlic and sauté until fragrant, about 1 minute.

3. Add shrimp to skillet and sauté until opaque in center, about 5 minutes. Transfer to a small bowl.

1. **To make Avocado Purée:** Scoop avocado flesh into a small food processor or blender. Add yogurt, lime juice, spinach, oil, salt, cumin, and chili powder. Purée.

1. **To make Tacos:** Top tortillas with shrimp, Avocado Purée, and cilantro. Enjoy.

PER SERVING

Calories: 1,235	Fiber: 18g
Fat: 86g	Carbohydrates: 85g
Protein: 37g	Sugar: 10g
Sodium: 2,449mg	

BAKED CATFISH

SERVES 1 | PREP: 10 MINUTES | COOK: 40 MINUTES

 This healthy Baked Catfish is sure to delight! The fish cooks along with vegetables in one pan for less time spent doing dishes afterward. While this recipe uses catfish, other firm fish such as cod and flounder will work well too.

INGREDIENTS

2 tablespoons extra-virgin olive oil, divided

1 medium fennel bulb, washed, cored, and thinly sliced

½ medium red pepper, seeded and cut into thin strips

½ small yellow onion, peeled and thinly sliced

2 small plum tomatoes, sliced in half lengthwise

2 cloves garlic, peeled and minced

¼ teaspoon dried thyme

¼ teaspoon kosher salt, divided

⅛ teaspoon freshly ground black pepper

3 tablespoons dry white wine

1 (6-ounce) catfish fillet

1. Preheat oven to 400°F.

2. In an ungreased 9.5" baking dish, toss together 1 tablespoon oil, fennel slices, red pepper slices, onion slices, tomatoes, garlic, thyme, ⅛ teaspoon salt, and pepper.

3. Place dish in oven and bake 20 minutes.

4. Remove dish from oven and stir in wine. Place catfish over vegetables and top with 1 tablespoon oil and remaining salt.

5. Place dish back in oven and bake 20 minutes more, until catfish is cooked through. Enjoy.

Smart Shopping Tip

Consider purchasing boxed wine. Once opened, bottles of wine can go bad after a few days. Boxed wine has an airtight inner bag that prevents exposure to oxygen even after the box is opened, so it can last up to a month.

PER SERVING

Calories: 617
Fat: 39g
Protein: 34g
Sodium: 899mg

Fiber: 11g
Carbohydrates: 33g
Sugar: 17g

VEGETARIAN MAIN DISHES

Years ago I started preparing meat-free dishes when my son became a vegetarian. At first it seemed difficult and honestly pretty limiting, since it significantly changed the options for what I could make. Over time, however, I discovered how many great protein alternatives there were, and just how much my experiences in the kitchen could be opened up by this new form of cooking. And, while I wasn't a vegetarian myself, I also started to see the great effects that swapping out some of my meat dishes for vegetarian ones was having on my health. After about six months my son started eating meat again, but I continued to incorporate vegetarian dishes in our everyday meals.

The recipes in this chapter include many of the favorites I have cultivated since making that switch to more vegetarian meals, such as Eggplant Parmesan and Chickpea Curry. Whether you are a vegetarian yourself, or are simply looking to change up your meals once in a while, you're sure to love the recipes in this chapter. From Caprese Pasta to the Spinach and Cheese Quesadilla, you'll soon forget they are meat-free!

CHICKPEA CURRY

SERVES 1 | PREP: 5 MINUTES | COOK: 25 MINUTES

 This wonderful Chickpea Curry is made with canned beans and canned coconut milk, so it's easy to prepare—but still filled with flavor. Since you'll use just ¾ cup of the coconut milk, refrigerate the rest and use it in a smoothie, add it to overnight oats, or stir it into your morning coffee.

INGREDIENTS

1 tablespoon olive oil

¼ cup peeled and chopped yellow onion

1 clove garlic, peeled and minced

1 teaspoon curry powder

⅛ teaspoon ground ginger

⅛ teaspoon kosher salt

½ cup vegetable broth

¾ cup canned coconut milk

½ tablespoon pure honey

1 (15-ounce) can chickpeas, drained and rinsed

1 cup cooked white rice

1. In a 10″ skillet over medium heat, heat oil 30 seconds. Add onions and cook 2 minutes, stirring occasionally, until onions soften. Add garlic, curry powder, ginger, and salt and stir, cooking an additional 1 minute.

2. Pour in vegetable broth, coconut milk, and honey and bring to a boil over high heat.

3. Once boiling, add chickpeas and reduce heat to low. Simmer 15 minutes, stirring occasionally, until slightly thickened.

4. Enjoy over rice on a medium plate.

PER SERVING

Calories: 790
Fat: 25g
Protein: 25g
Sodium: 1,193mg

Fiber: 19g
Carbohydrates: 121g
Sugar: 22g

TWICE-BAKED EGGPLANT

SERVES 1 | PREP: 30 MINUTES | COOK: 40 MINUTES

So creamy and delicious, this cheese-stuffed eggplant recipe will make an eggplant lover out of anyone!

INGREDIENTS

2 tablespoons olive oil, divided

½ teaspoon kosher salt, divided

¼ teaspoon freshly ground black pepper, divided

1 medium eggplant (about 1½ pounds), stem removed, cut in half lengthwise

¾ cup peeled and chopped yellow onion

2 cloves garlic, peeled and minced

2 cups shredded Cheddar cheese

½ cup grated Parmesan cheese

½ teaspoon dried oregano

2 tablespoons chopped fresh basil

1 large egg, beaten

1. Preheat oven to 375°F.

2. Drizzle 1 tablespoon oil, ¼ teaspoon salt, and ⅛ teaspoon pepper over both halves of eggplant. Place cut-side up on an ungreased baking sheet.

3. Bake eggplant 15 minutes. Remove from oven to cool 15 minutes.

4. Reduce oven to 350°F.

5. When eggplant is cool enough to handle, scoop eggplant out of skins, taking care not to damage skin. Cut eggplant into cubes. Set aside both cubes and skins.

6. In a 10" skillet over medium heat, heat 1 tablespoon oil 30 seconds. Add onions and garlic and cook until soft, about 3 minutes.

7. Add eggplant cubes and cook 5 minutes, then remove skillet from heat and set aside.

8. In a large bowl, mix together Cheddar cheese, Parmesan cheese, oregano, basil, remaining salt and pepper, and egg. Stir in eggplant mixture.

9. Spoon mixture into eggplant skins and transfer to a 9.5" baking dish lightly greased with butter or oil.

10. Bake eggplant 40 minutes. Allow to cool 5 minutes before transferring to a medium plate and serving.

PER SERVING

Calories: 1,588   Fiber: 17g
Fat: 119g   Carbohydrates: 55g
Protein: 80g   Sugar: 24g
Sodium: 3,406mg

CAPRESE TOAST

SERVES 1 | PREP: 10 MINUTES | COOK: 15 MINUTES

Bring a bit of Italy to your kitchen! Easy, cheesy, and absolutely delicious, this small-batch recipe can also be made in a toaster oven.

INGREDIENTS

4 slices Italian bread

5 fresh basil leaves, chopped (about 2 tablespoons), divided

1 cup ricotta cheese

¼ cup grated Parmesan cheese

¼ teaspoon kosher salt

⅛ teaspoon freshly ground black pepper

9 cherry tomatoes, halved

1 clove garlic, peeled and minced

1 tablespoon olive oil

½ teaspoon balsamic vinegar

4 ounces (about ½ cup) mozzarella cheese, sliced

1. Preheat oven to 425°F.

2. Place bread on ungreased baking sheet and toast on one side until golden, about 8 minutes.

3. In a small bowl, mix together ½ basil, ricotta, Parmesan cheese, salt, and pepper. Set aside.

4. In another small bowl, mix together tomatoes, garlic, oil, and balsamic vinegar. Set aside.

5. Spread ¼ ricotta mixture on one side of each bread slice. Top with 1 slice of mozzarella cheese. Spoon ¼ tomato mixture over mozzarella. Repeat with remaining bread slices.

6. Place bread on ungreased baking sheet and bake 9 minutes until heated through and mozzarella is melted.

7. Garnish with remaining basil and enjoy immediately.

PER SERVING

Calories: 1,227   Fiber: 5g
Fat: 80g   Carbohydrates: 59g
Protein: 69g   Sugar: 9g
Sodium: 2,289mg

MUSHROOM AND HERB CRUSTLESS QUICHE

SERVES 1 | PREP: 10 MINUTES | COOK: 25 MINUTES

 A quiche is a wonderfully adaptable dish. You can choose the current season's most flavorful vegetables, and any variety of cheeses and meats you prefer. Just keep the amounts of milk and eggs the same, then experiment with your other ingredients.

INGREDIENTS

½ tablespoon room temperature butter

½ tablespoon olive oil

½ cup sliced mushrooms

¼ cup peeled and chopped yellow onion

1 clove garlic, peeled and minced

¼ teaspoon dried thyme

2 large eggs

4 tablespoons heavy cream

¼ teaspoon kosher salt

⅛ teaspoon freshly ground black pepper

½ cup shredded Gruyère cheese

1. Preheat oven to 375°F. Butter a 5" × 5" baking dish and set aside.

2. In a 10" skillet over medium heat, add butter and oil and heat 30 seconds. Add mushrooms, onions, and garlic and cook, stirring frequently, until mushrooms are fork-tender, about 5 minutes. Stir in thyme and remove skillet from heat.

3. In a small bowl, whisk together eggs and cream. Stir in salt, pepper, mushroom mixture, and cheese.

4. Pour mixture into baking dish and bake until quiche is puffed and golden, 25 minutes. Slice and enjoy.

PER SERVING

Calories: 710   Fiber: 1g
Fat: 61g   Carbohydrates: 9g
Protein: 32g   Sugar: 5g
Sodium: 1,130mg

SKILLET RATATOUILLE

SERVES 1 | PREP: 10 MINUTES | COOK: 15 MINUTES

 This humble vegetable stew is a lovely meal for one that can be enjoyed with a glass of sauvignon blanc or served as a side to chicken or fish. Be sure to cut your vegetables into uniformly sized pieces to ensure they cook at the same rate.

INGREDIENTS

1 tablespoon olive oil

½ small yellow onion, peeled and thinly sliced

1 small zucchini, quartered lengthwise, cut into thin slices

1 medium red bell pepper, chopped and seeded

⅛ teaspoon kosher salt

1 medium Roma tomato, coarsely chopped

1 clove garlic, peeled and minced

¼ teaspoon dried basil

⅛ teaspoon dried oregano

⅛ teaspoon dried thyme

⅛ teaspoon freshly ground black pepper

1 tablespoon grated Parmesan cheese

1. In a 10" skillet over medium-high heat, heat oil 30 seconds. Add onions, zucchini, red peppers, and salt, and cook 8 minutes until vegetables are slightly tender.

2. Stir in tomatoes, garlic, and spices and cook, stirring occasionally, an additional 5 minutes.

3. Transfer to a medium plate and top with Parmesan cheese. Enjoy.

PER SERVING

Calories: 237
Fat: 16g
Protein: 6g
Sodium: 396mg

Fiber: 5g
Carbohydrates: 20g
Sugar: 11g

CHILI CHEESE BAKED POTATO

SERVES 1 | PREP: 10 MINUTES | COOK: 50 MINUTES

 This flavorful stuffed baked potato is an example of how kitchen staples can elevate a simple dish. Loaded with sautéed onions and garlic, beans, tomatoes, and spices, then topped with shredded Cheddar cheese and sour cream, it's a hearty vegetarian meal! Try substituting what you already have in your own pantry or refrigerator, from black beans and paprika to diced red pepper.

INGREDIENTS

1 medium russet potato, washed, patted dry, and pricked all over with a fork

¼ tablespoon softened butter

½ tablespoon olive oil

½ cup peeled and chopped yellow onion

1 clove garlic, peeled and minced

¼ teaspoon chili powder

⅛ teaspoon kosher salt

¼ cup canned red beans, rinsed and drained

¼ cup canned diced tomatoes, drained

1 tablespoon shredded Cheddar cheese

1 tablespoon sour cream

1. Preheat oven to 425°F. Rub potato with butter and place on an ungreased baking sheet.

2. Bake potato 40 minutes until tender. Remove from oven and set aside on a medium plate.

3. In an 8" skillet over medium-high heat, heat oil 30 seconds. Add onion and cook until softened, about 3 minutes. Add garlic and cook another 30 seconds.

4. Add chili powder and salt to skillet. Cook, stirring frequently, 1 minute. Add beans and tomatoes and continue cooking and stirring until heated through, about 2 minutes. Remove from heat.

5. Cut slit in top of potato; squeeze sides to open. Spoon bean mixture into slit of potato. Sprinkle with cheese and sour cream and enjoy.

Storing Butter
Butter can be stored in the freezer for up to six months. Keep what you will use quickly in the refrigerator and freeze the rest.

PER SERVING

Calories: 380
Fat: 15g
Protein: 10g
Sodium: 486mg

Fiber: 10g
Carbohydrates: 53g
Sugar: 8g

BAKED PASTA
WITH ROASTED VEGETABLES

SERVES 1 | PREP: 25 MINUTES | COOK: 25 MINUTES

 This easy-to-make baked pasta is a small-batch recipe bursting with flavor! One thing I love about this dish is that you can change up the vegetables based on what you have on hand. And while it calls for smoked Gruyère and fontina cheeses, you can use other creamy cheese options like smoked mozzarella or Brie.

INGREDIENTS

½ cup diced zucchini

½ cup diced, seeded red bell peppers

½ cup peeled and chopped yellow onion

1 clove garlic, peeled and minced

2 tablespoons olive oil

¼ teaspoon herbs de Provence

⅛ teaspoon kosher salt

⅛ teaspoon freshly ground black pepper

⅔ cup penne pasta, cooked al dente according to package instructions

¾ cup marinara sauce

¼ cup shredded fontina cheese

¼ cup shredded smoked Gruyère cheese

2 tablespoons grated Parmesan cheese

1 tablespoon cold butter, cut into small pieces

1. Preheat oven to 450°F.

2. On a large, ungreased baking sheet, toss zucchini, peppers, onions, and garlic with oil, spices, salt, and pepper.

3. Place baking sheet in the oven and roast until tender, about 15 minutes.

4. In a medium bowl, toss cooked pasta with roasted vegetables, marinara sauce, and all cheeses except Parmesan.

5. Pour pasta into a 5" × 5" baking dish greased with butter or oil. Top with Parmesan and butter, and bake until top is golden and cheese melts, about 25 minutes.

6. Transfer pasta to a medium bowl and enjoy.

PER SERVING

Calories: 1,012
Fat: 64g
Protein: 33g
Sodium: 1,951mg

Fiber: 10g
Carbohydrates: 78g
Sugar: 19g

CAPRESE PASTA

SERVES 1 | PREP: 5 MINUTES | COOK: 15 MINUTES

 This Caprese Pasta is made with fresh mozzarella cheese, ripe tomatoes, and pasta. It cooks quickly and makes a hearty single-serving meal. Though the recipe calls for rotini, feel free to use any kind of pasta you like.

INGREDIENTS

1 tablespoon olive oil

1 medium Roma tomato, seeded and chopped into ½" pieces

⅛ teaspoon kosher salt

1 clove garlic, peeled and minced

½ cup (about 2 ounces) rotini pasta, cooked according to package instructions

½ cup shredded mozzarella cheese

½ teaspoon grated Parmesan cheese

2 fresh basil leaves, torn

1. In a 10" skillet over medium-high heat, heat oil 30 seconds. Add tomatoes and salt and cook, stirring frequently until tomatoes have softened, 2 minutes.

2. Add garlic and cook, stirring constantly, 1 minute longer. Stir in pasta, mozzarella, Parmesan, and basil and toss to coat.

3. Transfer to a medium plate and serve immediately.

PER SERVING

Calories: 524
Fat: 28g
Protein: 21g
Sodium: 841mg

Fiber: 3g
Carbohydrates: 47g
Sugar: 3g

SPINACH PESTO PASTA

SERVES 1 | PREP: 10 MINUTES | COOK: 10 MINUTES

 Quick and easy pasta with fresh pesto for the win! Pesto is easy to make for any occasion: Just add the ingredients to a food processor and pulse until puréed. Stir this pesto into pasta, or enjoy over chicken or fish, or portioned as a side.

INGREDIENTS

4 cups fresh spinach leaves, loosely packed

½ cup toasted pine nuts

2 cloves garlic, peeled and chopped

1 tablespoon lemon juice

⅓ cup olive oil

½ cup shredded Parmesan cheese

⅛ teaspoon kosher salt

2 ounces penne, cooked according to instructions

1. Add spinach, pine nuts, garlic, and lemon juice to a food processor. Lightly pulse. While machine is running, gradually add oil until mixture is creamy. Add Parmesan and salt and pulse again.

2. Pour over cooked pasta in a medium bowl and enjoy.

PER SERVING

Calories: 1,506   Fiber: 7g
Fat: 130g   Carbohydrates: 59g
Protein: 35g   Sugar: 4g
Sodium: 1,219mg

CHEESY VEGETARIAN PASTA BAKE

SERVES 1 | PREP: 10 MINUTES | COOK: 30 MINUTES

This pasta bake is a hearty, healthy meal that can also be made with any leftover pasta from a previous meal. Also feel free to substitute other vegetables for the ones used.

INGREDIENTS

2 cups cooked rotini pasta

¼ cup frozen corn

¼ cup frozen green beans

1 cup spaghetti sauce, divided

½ teaspoon dried basil

⅛ teaspoon kosher salt

⅛ teaspoon freshly ground black pepper

1 cup mozzarella cheese, divided

1. Preheat oven to 350°F.

2. Place pasta in a large bowl. Add corn, green beans, ½ cup sauce, dried basil, salt, pepper, and ½ cup mozzarella cheese. Stir well.

3. Pour pasta mixture into a 5" × 5" baking dish lightly greased with butter or oil. Top with remaining sauce and mozzarella cheese.

4. Bake 30 minutes until cheese is melted. Enjoy immediately.

PER SERVING

Calories: 862   Fiber: 11g

Fat: 32g   Carbohydrates: 100g

Protein: 44g   Sugar: 18g

Sodium: 2,453mg

EGGPLANT PARMESAN

SERVES 1 | PREP: 10 MINUTES | COOK: 30 MINUTES

 This is the very best-tasting Eggplant Parmesan! In fact, my husband won't order Eggplant Parmesan at a restaurant anymore because he knows it won't be as good as this one. Pair with a side salad, or enjoy alone.

INGREDIENTS

1 large egg, lightly beaten

½ cup plain bread crumbs

¼ cup shredded vegetarian Parmesan cheese

½ teaspoon dried basil

½ teaspoon kosher salt

¼ teaspoon dried oregano

¼ teaspoon garlic powder

¼ teaspoon freshly ground black pepper

1 small eggplant (about ¾ pound), peeled and sliced into ¼" slices

1 tablespoon olive oil

1 cup shredded vegetarian mozzarella cheese

¾ cup tomato sauce

2 tablespoons grated vegetarian Parmesan cheese

1. Preheat oven to 350°F.

2. Place egg in a small dish.

3. In a separate small bowl, stir together bread crumbs, Parmesan cheese, dried basil, salt, dried oregano, garlic powder, and pepper.

4. Dip 1 eggplant slice in egg, letting excess egg drip off, then dredge in bread crumb mixture until evenly coated, shaking off excess. Place on a large sheet of wax paper. Repeat with remaining eggplant.

5. In a medium skillet over medium-high heat, heat oil 30 seconds. Add 3 eggplant slices and fry 5 minutes until golden, turning over once halfway through frying. Transfer to a large paper towel–lined plate to drain. Repeat with remaining eggplant slices.

6. Arrange ½ eggplant in a layer on bottom of a 5" × 5" baking dish greased with cooking spray.

7. Cover eggplant with ½ mozzarella cheese and ½ tomato sauce. Repeat layering with remaining eggplant, mozzarella, and sauce. Sprinkle with Parmesan cheese.

8. Bake 30 minutes until cheese has melted. Enjoy.

Is All Parmesan Cheese Vegetarian?

Sometimes Parmesan cheese is not vegetarian because it has been made using animal rennet (an enzyme used to set cheese). Check to make sure that the Parmesan cheese you buy is made with vegetarian rennet, choose a dairy-free version, or substitute with nutritional yeast.

PER SERVING

Calories: 912
Fat: 54g
Protein: 52g
Sodium: 3,020mg

Fiber: 12g
Carbohydrates: 60g
Sugar: 19g

PASTA WITH POMODORO SAUCE

SERVES 1 | PREP: 5 MINUTES | COOK: 15 MINUTES

 Pomodoro sauce is a flavorful Italian sauce made with garlic, tomatoes, and spices. You can certainly make pomodoro sauce with fresh tomatoes, but I love using canned tomatoes because I always have a can in my pantry and it makes the recipe that much easier.

INGREDIENTS

1 (14-ounce) can whole tomatoes, including juice

½ tablespoon olive oil

1 clove garlic, peeled and minced

¼ teaspoon dried basil

¼ teaspoon kosher salt

⅛ teaspoon freshly ground black pepper

1½ tablespoons pure honey

1 cup cooked vermicelli pasta

1. Pour tomatoes into a blender and pulse to form a coarse purée.

2. In a medium saucepan over medium-high heat, heat oil 30 seconds. Add garlic and cook until it begins to brown, 1 minute.

3. Add tomato purée and season with dried basil, salt, and pepper. Stir in honey.

4. Bring to a boil over high heat, then reduce heat to low and simmer 15 minutes, until slightly thickened.

5. Spoon sauce over pasta in a medium bowl and enjoy.

PER SERVING

Calories: 445
Fat: 9g
Protein: 12g
Sodium: 1,365mg

Fiber: 9g
Carbohydrates: 84g
Sugar: 35g

SPAGHETTI AGLIO E OLIO

SERVES 1 | PREP: 5 MINUTES | COOK: 20 MINUTES

 Spaghetti Aglio E Olio is said to have been created by Italian farmers who had nothing but the most basic of Italian ingredients on hand. Using those humble items, they were able to transform a simple plate of pasta into an incredibly delicious meal—and now you can too!

INGREDIENTS

2 ounces dry spaghetti (about 2⅛" circumference)

1 tablespoon olive oil, divided

1 clove garlic, peeled and minced

⅛ teaspoon cayenne pepper

1 tablespoon chopped fresh parsley

1 tablespoon Parmesan cheese

1. Bring a 2-quart pot of salted water to a boil over high heat. Add pasta and cook until al dente, about 9 minutes. Drain pasta, reserving ½ cup cooking liquid, and set aside in a medium bowl.

2. In a 10" skillet over medium-low heat, heat ½ tablespoon oil 30 seconds. Add garlic and cook until lightly browned, about 2 minutes.

3. Add reserved cooking liquid to skillet and stir in cayenne pepper. Bring to a simmer over medium-high heat, and cook until liquid is reduced by half, about 5 minutes.

4. Add cooked pasta to skillet and toss continuously until sauce thickens and coats pasta, 1 minute.

5. Remove skillet from heat and stir in parsley and remaining ½ tablespoon olive oil.

6. Spoon into a medium bowl, top with Parmesan cheese, and enjoy immediately.

PER SERVING

Calories: 423
Fat: 23g
Protein: 10g
Sodium: 269mg

Fiber: 3g
Carbohydrates: 44g
Sugar: 1g

TOMATO BISQUE

SERVES 1 | PREP: 10 MINUTES | COOK: 35 MINUTES

 A traditional bisque is made with seafood stock, but the modern usage of the word can mean any puréed soup made with cream. This wonderful Tomato Bisque is a velvety-smooth version of classic tomato soup, with a touch of heavy cream added at the end. Enjoy with a piece of crusty French bread.

INGREDIENTS

½ tablespoon olive oil

¼ cup peeled and chopped yellow onion

¼ cup chopped celery

1 clove garlic, peeled and minced

¼ teaspoon smoked paprika

¼ teaspoon kosher salt

⅛ teaspoon freshly ground black pepper

1 (14-ounce) can diced tomatoes, including juice

½ cup vegetable broth

1 teaspoon pure honey

2 tablespoons heavy cream

1. In a 2-quart pot over medium heat, heat oil 30 seconds. Add onions and celery and cook until onions are translucent, about 3 minutes.

2. Add garlic, smoked paprika, salt, and pepper and cook, stirring frequently, an additional 1 minute.

3. Add tomatoes and broth and bring to a boil over high heat, then reduce heat to low and simmer, stirring occasionally, 20 minutes.

4. Stir in honey and transfer soup to a stand blender, or use an immersion blender to purée.

5. Return soup to pot and stir in cream. Pour into a medium bowl and enjoy immediately.

PER SERVING

Calories: 342   Fiber: 9g
Fat: 19g   Carbohydrates: 43g
Protein: 9g   Sugar: 27g
Sodium: 1,678mg

BLACK BEAN SOUP

SERVES 1 | PREP: 10 MINUTES | COOK: 35 MINUTES

 This fresh-tasting Black Bean Soup is made with ingredients you may already have on hand, and comes together easily. You might like to add a dollop of sour cream, chopped fresh cilantro, or grated cotija cheese to your bowl after it's cooked.

INGREDIENTS

½ tablespoon olive oil

¼ cup peeled and chopped yellow onion

1 medium stalk celery, finely chopped

⅛ teaspoon kosher salt

1 clove garlic, peeled and minced

½ teaspoon ground cumin

⅛ teaspoon cayenne pepper

1 (15-ounce) can black beans, rinsed and drained

1 cup vegetable broth

1. In a 1-quart saucepan over medium heat, heat oil 30 seconds. Add onions, celery, and salt. Cook, stirring occasionally, until vegetables are soft, about 8 minutes.

2. Stir in garlic, cumin, and cayenne pepper and cook, stirring frequently, 30 seconds.

3. Pour in beans and broth and bring to a boil over high heat, then reduce heat to medium-low and simmer until beans are very tender, about 20 minutes.

4. Transfer soup to a stand blender and blend until smooth, or use an immersion blender to blend the soup.

5. Pour soup into a medium bowl and enjoy while hot.

PER SERVING

Calories: 444
Fat: 10g
Protein: 22g
Sodium: 1,603mg

Fiber: 2g
Carbohydrates: 69g
Sugar: 3g

VEGETARIAN TORTILLA SOUP

SERVES 1 | PREP: 10 MINUTES | COOK: 30 MINUTES

 A hearty and satisfying meal for one, this Vegetarian Tortilla Soup comes together quickly and easily. It's loaded with plenty of chopped onions, sweet red peppers, and corn. Feel free to top your bowl with shredded Cheddar cheese and crushed tortilla chips.

INGREDIENTS

½ tablespoon olive oil

¼ cup peeled and chopped yellow onion

¼ cup chopped and seeded red peppers

1 clove garlic, peeled and minced

½ teaspoon ground cumin

¼ teaspoon kosher salt

⅛ teaspoon freshly ground black pepper

¾ cup canned diced tomatoes (about ½ of a 15-ounce can), including juice

1 cup vegetable broth

¼ cup frozen whole kernel corn

1. In a 2-quart saucepan over medium heat, heat oil 30 seconds. Add onions and peppers and cook 4 minutes, stirring occasionally.

2. Add garlic, cumin, salt, and pepper, and cook, stirring frequently, 1 minute.

3. Add tomatoes and broth and bring to a boil over high heat, then reduce heat to low and simmer 15 minutes.

4. Stir in corn and cook another 5 minutes, then pour into a medium bowl and enjoy immediately.

PER SERVING

Calories: 195   Fiber: 6g
Fat: 8g   Carbohydrates: 30g
Protein: 6g   Sugar: 13g
Sodium: 1,580mg

CHIPS AND QUESO

SERVES 1 | PREP: 10 MINUTES | COOK: 15 MINUTES

 This white queso, also known as *queso blanco*, is creamy, easy to make, and made with just three ingredients. This is a dip you'll want to make over and over again— both as a side and as a full meal.

INGREDIENTS

For Chips

3 (10") flour tortillas, cut into 6 equal-sized wedges

2 teaspoons olive oil

⅛ teaspoon kosher salt

For Queso

¼ pound white American cheese

¼ cup half-and-half

1 tablespoon salsa verde

1. **To make Chips:** Preheat oven to 350°F.

2. Brush both sides of each tortilla wedge with oil and place on an ungreased baking sheet. Sprinkle with salt.

3. Place baking sheet in oven and bake 10 minutes, rotating the sheet after 4 minutes so tortilla wedges brown evenly.

4. Remove sheet from oven and let cool 5 minutes. When cool enough to handle, place tortilla chips in a medium bowl. Set aside.

1. **To make Queso:** Place cheese, half-and-half, and salsa verde in a small pan over medium heat. Cook, stirring occasionally, until cheese has melted and queso is smooth, about 5 minutes.

2. Enjoy queso immediately with chips.

PER SERVING

Calories: 1,240   Fiber: 8g
Fat: 69g   Carbohydrates: 116g
Protein: 37g   Sugar: 17g
Sodium: 3,882mg

SPINACH AND CHEESE QUESADILLA

SERVES 1 | PREP: 5 MINUTES | COOK: 10 MINUTES

Quesadillas are a wonderful alternative to sandwiches; they're easy to prepare and are made with just a few simple ingredients. For this Spinach and Cheese Quesadilla, feel free to substitute different cheeses.

INGREDIENTS

2 (8") flour tortillas

2 deli slices pepper jack cheese

½ cup fresh spinach leaves

1. Heat a 10" nonstick skillet over medium-high heat 30 seconds. Place 1 tortilla in skillet. Evenly arrange cheese slices over tortilla. Add spinach and place second tortilla on top.

2. Heat quesadilla 3 minutes, then flip and cook another 3 minutes until cheese is melted.

3. Remove from pan and cut into wedges. Enjoy warm.

PER SERVING

Calories: 481 | Fat: 19g | Protein: 17g | Sodium: 757mg
Fiber: 3g | Carbohydrates: 59g | Sugar: 0g

SPICY STIR-FRIED ZUCCHINI

SERVES 1 | PREP: 5 MINUTES | COOK: 5 MINUTES

This Spicy Stir-Fried Zucchini is made with just a few ingredients and takes minutes to make. Enjoy with rice, or enjoy on its own.

INGREDIENTS

1 tablespoon olive oil

1 medium zucchini, cut into ½" pieces

¼ teaspoon kosher salt

⅛ teaspoon freshly ground black pepper

⅛ teaspoon ground ginger

2 teaspoons Thai Kitchen Sweet Red Chili Sauce

½ teaspoon sesame seeds

1. In a 10" skillet over medium-high heat, heat oil 30 seconds. Add zucchini, salt, pepper, ginger, and sauce. Stir-fry until crisp-tender, about 2 minutes.

2. Transfer to a medium bowl and stir in sesame seeds.

3. Let cool to room temperature, about 10 minutes and enjoy.

PER SERVING

Calories: 189 | Fat: 15g | Protein: 3g | Sodium: 698mg
Fiber: 2g | Carbohydrates: 11g | Sugar: 8g

VEGETARIAN CHILI

SERVES 1 | PREP: 10 MINUTES | COOK: 30 MINUTES

 This Vegetarian Chili is a wonderful alternative to traditional chili. It's made with canned cannellini (garbanzo) beans and filled with flavor. Enjoy with a dollop of sour cream, a hefty sprinkling of shredded Cheddar cheese, and fresh chopped cilantro.

INGREDIENTS

½ tablespoon olive oil

¼ cup peeled and chopped yellow onion

2 tablespoons chopped and seeded green bell pepper

1 small zucchini, diced

1 clove garlic, peeled and minced

1 (15-ounce) can cannellini beans, rinsed and drained

1 (15-ounce) can diced tomatoes, including juice

⅛ teaspoon chili powder

⅛ teaspoon kosher salt

1. In a 10" skillet over medium-high heat, heat oil 30 seconds. Add onions, peppers, and zucchini and cook, stirring occasionally, 5 minutes.

2. Add garlic and cook, stirring frequently, 30 seconds.

3. Stir in beans, diced tomatoes, chili powder, and salt, and bring to a boil over high heat. Once boiling, reduce heat to low and simmer uncovered 15 minutes.

4. Spoon into a medium bowl and serve immediately.

PER SERVING

Calories: 552   Fiber: 26g
Fat: 11g   Carbohydrates: 94g
Protein: 30g   Sugar: 24g
Sodium: 1,634mg

ONE-POT VEGETARIAN CHILI MAC

SERVES 1 | PREP: 10 MINUTES | COOK: 20 MINUTES

 In this flavorful One-Pot Vegetarian Chili Mac, I've brought together two favorite meals: chili and pasta. Made with plenty of vegetables, canned red (or black if preferred) beans, and a glorious assortment of spices, it can be ready and on your table in under 30 minutes.

INGREDIENTS

1 tablespoon olive oil

¼ cup peeled and chopped yellow onion

¼ cup chopped and seeded red bell peppers

1 clove garlic, peeled and minced

1 teaspoon tomato paste

½ cup vegetable broth

¼ cup canned red beans, rinsed and drained

½ teaspoon ground cumin

¼ teaspoon kosher salt

⅛ teaspoon chili powder

½ cup (about 2 ounces) macaroni pasta

1 tablespoon Parmesan cheese

1. In a 10" skillet over medium-high heat, heat oil 30 seconds. Add onions and peppers and cook, stirring occasionally, 4 minutes until tender.

2. Add garlic and tomato paste and cook, stirring frequently, 1 minute.

3. Pour in vegetable broth, beans, cumin, salt, and chili powder and bring to a boil over high heat, then reduce heat to medium-low, add pasta, and cover pot.

4. Continue cooking, stirring occasionally, 15 minutes, until pasta is tender.

5. Transfer to a medium bowl, top with Parmesan cheese, and enjoy immediately.

Storing Tomato Paste
To store leftover tomato paste, freeze it in ice cube trays. When frozen, pop the cubes out of the tray and store in a zip-top bag in the freezer.

PER SERVING

Calories: 418
Fat: 17g
Protein: 13g
Sodium: 1,062mg

Fiber: 6g
Carbohydrates: 54g
Sugar: 5g

VEGETARIAN ENCHILADAS VERDES

SERVES 1 | PREP: 10 MINUTES | COOK: 15 MINUTES

 Instead of filling and rolling the tortillas, the ingredients are layered, casserole-style in a 5" × 5" baking dish. They can be made with jarred tomatillo sauce or salsa—your choice—and you might also consider topping with sour cream, sliced jalapeños, and chopped cilantro for extra flavor.

INGREDIENTS

¼ cup canola oil

3 (8") corn tortillas

1 small zucchini, diced

⅛ teaspoon kosher salt

4 ounces tomatillo sauce

¼ cup shredded Monterey jack cheese

1. Preheat oven to 350°F.

2. In a 10" skillet over medium heat, add oil and heat 30 seconds. Add tortillas one at a time to soften, 20 seconds each. Set aside warm tortillas on a large paper towel–lined plate.

3. Turn heat to medium-high and add zucchini and salt. Cook, stirring frequently, 5 minutes until zucchini is fork-tender. Transfer to a medium bowl and set aside.

4. To assemble enchiladas, place 1 ounce tomatillo sauce on bottom of an ungreased 5" × 5" baking dish. Place 1 tortilla on top, then top with ½ zucchini and sprinkle with 2 tablespoons cheese.

5. Place another tortilla on top of cheese and repeat with remaining zucchini and 1 tablespoon cheese.

6. Place last tortilla on top, cover with remaining tomatillo sauce, and top with remaining cheese.

7. Place dish in oven and bake 15 minutes until cheese has melted. Slice and enjoy.

PER SERVING

Calories: 990

Fat: 75g

Protein: 15g

Sodium: 1,163mg

Fiber: 8g

Carbohydrates: 68g

Sugar: 7g

POTATO AND ASPARAGUS CRUSTLESS QUICHE

SERVES 1 | PREP: 20 MINUTES | COOK: 25 MINUTES

 No crust is necessary with this lovely Potato and Asparagus Crustless Quiche. Potatoes, asparagus, onions, and garlic are roasted to perfection then mixed with eggs, cream, and fontina cheese. It's a single-serving quiche perfect for brunch or dinner.

INGREDIENTS

¾ cup diced red potatoes

¾ cup chopped fresh asparagus, woody ends removed

½ cup peeled and sliced yellow onion

2 cloves garlic, peeled and chopped

1 tablespoon olive oil

½ teaspoon kosher salt, divided

¼ teaspoon freshly ground black pepper, divided

2 large eggs

4 tablespoons heavy cream

½ cup shredded fontina cheese

1. Preheat oven to 400°F.

2. Spread potatoes, asparagus, onions, and garlic on an ungreased baking sheet. Top with oil, ¼ teaspoon salt, and ⅛ teaspoon black pepper. Gently toss to combine.

3. Place baking sheet in oven and bake 14 minutes until tender.

4. Remove from oven and set aside, then reduce oven temperature to 350°F.

5. In a medium mixing bowl, whisk together eggs, cream, and remaining salt and pepper. Stir in cheese.

6. Gently fold in roasted vegetables and pour into a 5" × 5" baking dish lightly greased with butter or oil.

7. Place in oven and bake until quiche is puffed and golden, about 25 minutes. Enjoy hot.

PER SERVING

Calories: 828   Fiber: 5g
Fat: 62g   Carbohydrates: 37g
Protein: 34g   Sugar: 9g
Sodium: 1,765mg

CHAPTER EIGHT

DESSERTS

Whether you are looking for a great way to finish a meal or satisfy a midday craving for something sweet, a great dessert is an indulgence that you deserve. Somedays dessert might even replace dinner. (Hey, no judgment here: been there, done that.) Of course, a lot of dessert recipes leave you stuck with tons of leftovers you don't want to feel tempted by, but also don't want to let go to waste. It can seem like a lose-lose situation—which is where we come in!

With the single-serving recipes in this chapter, you get the pleasure you crave *without* the guilt. From classic homemade Vanilla Ice Cream, to favorites like Pecan Pie, Rocky Road Fudge, and Lemon Bars, you're sure to discover the perfect recipe for satisfying that sweet tooth. And if you're looking to try something a little out of the ordinary, you'll love the Tres Leches Cake (a popular recipe from my hometown of Houston) and Bananas Foster.

PEACH CRISP

SERVES 1 | PREP: 10 MINUTES | COOK: 5 MINUTES

 This glorious Peach Crisp is made with just one fresh peach and a buttery crumb topping. You can use this basic crisp recipe with just about any stone fruit: apricots, nectarines, plums, and even cherries. It's easy to make and can be ready in minutes.

INGREDIENTS

For Filling

1 large peach, pitted and diced

1 tablespoon light brown sugar

1 teaspoon all-purpose flour

⅛ teaspoon ground ginger

For Topping

3 tablespoons all-purpose flour

3 tablespoons rolled oats

1 tablespoon light brown sugar

2 tablespoons butter, melted

Preheat oven to 350°F.

1. **To make Filling:** Mix together peaches, brown sugar, flour, and ginger in a small bowl.

2. Transfer mixture to a 5" × 5" baking dish or 8-ounce ramekin greased with cooking spray.

1. **To make Topping:** In another small bowl, mix together flour, oats, brown sugar, and melted butter.

2. Scatter topping evenly over peaches and bake 33 minutes until topping is golden. Enjoy warm.

What's the Difference Between Crisp, Crumble, and Cobbler?

It's easy to get confused by crisps, crumbles, and cobblers; they all seem so similar. However, there are differences between each dessert. A crisp is a fruit dessert with a streusel-like topping that contains oats. A crumble also contains fresh fruit with a streusel-like topping, but the topping is not made with oats. A cobbler has a biscuit topping over the fresh fruit.

PER SERVING

Calories: 553   Fiber: 5g

Fat: 25g   Carbohydrates: 78g

Protein: 7g   Sugar: 41g

Sodium: 12mg

STRAWBERRY SORBET

SERVES 1 | PREP: 10 MINUTES | COOK: 0 MINUTES

 This easy-to-make, refreshing sorbet is prepared with just three ingredients: strawberries, honey, and water, and is whipped up in a bowl. No ice cream maker needed! When fruit purée is frozen, it tastes less sweet than when unfrozen, hence the addition of honey for the perfect touch of sweetness. If you prefer your sorbet less sweet, you can leave out the honey altogether.

INGREDIENTS

2 cups chopped frozen strawberries

2 tablespoons pure honey

3 tablespoons water

1. Place strawberries, honey, and water in a blender and purée until smooth.

2. Pour strawberry juice into a medium freezer-safe container and freeze until firm, about 6 hours. Enjoy.

Stock Up

Keep bags of frozen fruits in your freezer. Frozen fruit can be just as nutritious as fresh, and it's nice to have fruit already on hand when you're ready to use it, especially when the fresh fruit isn't in season. Be sure to look for brands that do not contain any added sugar.

PER SERVING

Calories: 232
Fat: 0g
Protein: 1g
Sodium: 8mg

Fiber: 6g
Carbohydrates: 62g
Sugar: 48g

ORANGE POSSET

When you add an acid like citrus juice to milk, it causes the milk to sour or curdle. But when you add an acid to cream, the effect is entirely different; because cream has more fat and less water than milk, the texture becomes smooth and creamy.

INGREDIENTS

1 cup heavy cream

2 tablespoons granulated sugar

2 tablespoons pulp-free orange juice

¼ teaspoon vanilla extract

¼ teaspoon orange zest

1. Add cream and sugar to a small saucepan over medium heat. Slowly bring to a simmer and cook, stirring constantly to dissolve sugar, 7 minutes.

2. Remove pan from heat and stir in orange juice, vanilla, and orange zest. Let mixture steep 5 minutes.

3. Pour mixture into a ungreased 6- or 8-ounce ramekin. Cover and place in refrigerator to chill at least 4 hours before eating.

PER SERVING

*Calories: 931 | Fat: 87g | Protein: 7g | Sodium: 65mg
Fiber: 0g | Carbohydrates: 35g | Sugar: 34g*

VANILLA ICE CREAM

What if I told you that you can enjoy a decadent, smooth Vanilla Ice Cream by mixing together just three ingredients in one bowl? It's just the right amount for a large bowl to yourself, or two small bowls if you feel like sharing.

INGREDIENTS

½ cup heavy cream

¼ cup sweetened condensed milk

½ teaspoon vanilla extract

1. Pour cream into a medium bowl and whip until stiff peaks form. Gently fold in sweetened condensed milk and vanilla.

2. Pour mixture into a medium serving bowl, cover, and freeze at least 2 hours before eating.

PER SERVING

*Calories: 659 | Fat: 50g | Protein: 9g | Sodium: 130mg
Fiber: 0g | Carbohydrates: 45g | Sugar: 45g*

FUDGE RIPPLE ICE CREAM

SERVES 1 | PREP: 10 MINUTES | COOK: 0 MINUTES

This single-serving, egg-free ice cream is the perfect cure for your ice cream cravings—no ice cream maker and no cooking required. It's rich, creamy, and so easy to make!

INGREDIENTS

½ cup heavy cream

¼ cup sweetened condensed milk

½ teaspoon vanilla extract

1 tablespoon hot fudge sauce

1. Pour cream into a medium bowl and whip 2 minutes until stiff peaks form. Gently fold in sweetened condensed milk and vanilla.

2. Drizzle hot fudge over top, then take a large dull knife and swirl mixture a few times. Cover and freeze at least 2 hours until firm.

PER SERVING

Calories: 709 | Fat: 50g | Protein: 10g | Sodium: 137mg
Fiber: 1g | Carbohydrates: 57g | Sugar: 55g

BANANAS FOSTER

SERVES 1 | PREP: 5 MINUTES | COOK: 10 MINUTES

Bananas Foster is a famous New Orleans dessert made with sliced bananas, brown sugar, butter, and a bit of rum, served with vanilla ice cream. Typically, Bananas Foster is cooked tableside using a flambé, where the rum is dramatically set on fire, but don't worry: This flame isn't necessary!

INGREDIENTS

2 tablespoons room temperature butter

2 tablespoons packed light brown sugar

⅛ teaspoon ground cinnamon

1 tablespoon dark rum

1 medium ripe banana, peeled and sliced

1 cup vanilla ice cream

1. In an 8" skillet over medium heat, melt butter 30 seconds. Add brown sugar and cinnamon and cook, stirring frequently, 30 seconds. Add rum and banana slices and cook another 3 minutes.

2. Pour over ice cream in a medium bowl and enjoy immediately.

PER SERVING

Calories: 720 | Fat: 38g | Protein: 6g | Sodium: 118mg
Fiber: 4g | Carbohydrates: 85g | Sugar: 69g

DEEP-DISH CHOCOLATE CHIP COOKIE

SERVES 1 | PREP: 5 MINUTES | COOK: 25 MINUTES

 With buttery crisp edges and a warm, gooey center, this deep-dish chocolate chip cookie can be baked in a ramekin as directed in the recipe, or spooned onto a medium baking sheet and baked the traditional way. It's a totally indulgent treat for one.

INGREDIENTS

2 tablespoons butter, softened

2 tablespoons light brown sugar

1 tablespoon granulated sugar

1 large egg yolk

¼ teaspoon vanilla extract

⅓ cup all-purpose flour

⅛ teaspoon baking soda

⅛ teaspoon kosher salt

¼ cup semi-sweet chocolate chips

2 tablespoons chopped walnuts

1. Preheat oven to 350°F.

2. Mix together butter and sugars in a small mixing bowl. Add egg yolk and vanilla and continue mixing until well combined.

3. Add in flour, baking soda, and salt and stir until just combined. Fold in chocolate chips and chopped walnuts.

4. Pour cookie dough into an 8-ounce ramekin greased with butter or oil. Bake 24 minutes until top is golden and edges are set.

5. Remove from oven and place on a cooling rack to cool 10 minutes before eating.

PER SERVING

Calories: 567
Fat: 28g
Protein: 7g
Sodium: 468mg

Fiber: 1g
Carbohydrates: 72g
Sugar: 40g

LEMON MERINGUE PIE

SERVES 1 | PREP: 20 MINUTES | COOK: 20 MINUTES

 This luscious recipe is a scaled-down version of the classic lemon meringue pie. It uses a graham cracker crust because it is so simple to make, and tastes delicious paired with the pie filling.

INGREDIENTS

For Crust

½ cup (2 large sheets) crushed graham crackers

1 teaspoon granulated sugar

1 tablespoon butter, melted

For Filling

3 tablespoons granulated sugar

1 tablespoon cornstarch

⅓ cup water

1 large egg yolk

½ tablespoon butter

2 tablespoons lemon juice

½ teaspoon lemon zest

For Meringue

1 large egg white

⅛ teaspoon cream of tartar

1½ tablespoons granulated sugar

1. **To make Crust:** Preheat oven to 350°F.

2. Crush graham crackers by adding them to a food processor and pulsing until they resemble fine crumbs. Alternatively, place crackers in a zip-top plastic bag and crush with a rolling pin. Pour crumbs into a small bowl and stir in sugar and butter.

3. Grease the bottom and sides of a 4" ramekin with butter or cooking spray and pour crumb mixture into ramekin. Use your fingers or the back of a spoon to press crumbs gently to form a crust.

4. Bake 10 minutes. Remove from the oven and set aside.

1. **To make Filling:** Increase oven temperature to 400°F.

2. In a 1-quart saucepan over medium heat, mix sugar and cornstarch. Gradually stir in water. Cook, stirring constantly, until mixture thickens and begins to boil. Boil and stir 1 minute.

3. Stir 1 spoonful of hot mixture into egg yolk to temper yolk; stir yolk into hot mixture in saucepan. Continue to boil and stir constantly 2 minutes, then remove from heat.

4. Stir in butter, lemon juice, and lemon zest. Pour over pie crust.

PER SERVING

Calories: 697   Fiber: 2g
Fat: 27g   Carbohydrates: 110g
Protein: 6g   Sugar: 74g
Sodium: 243mg

LEMON MERINGUE PIE CONT.

1. **To make Meringue:** Beat egg white and cream of tartar with an electric mixer on high until foamy.

2. Beat in sugar, ½ tablespoon at a time; continue beating until stiff and glossy.

3. Spoon meringue onto pie filling. Spread evenly over filling, carefully sealing meringue to edge of crust to prevent "shrinking."

4. Bake until lightly golden brown, 11 minutes.

5. Let cool away from oven draft 1 hour, then cover and refrigerate until ready to enjoy.

The Secret to a Perfect Meringue

The perfect meringue should be light, fluffy, perfectly sweet and stiff. To make it at home, keep these key tips in mind:

- Make sure your bowl and whisk or beaters are absolutely clean.

- For best results, egg whites should be at room temperature before whipping.

- Make sure no egg yolk gets into the white, as it prevents the egg white from whipping up.

- Add the sugar to the egg white little by little. This gives the sugar time to fully dissolve.

NO-BAKE STRAWBERRY CHEESECAKE

SERVES 1 | PREP: 10 MINUTES + 20 MINUTES CHILL TIME | COOK: 0 MINUTES

 This is the perfect dessert to make when you crave a little something sweet. It takes just minutes to make, and you don't need to chill it before eating. If you choose to enjoy it without chilling it first, the gloriously creamy filling will be more mousse-like and less firm.

INGREDIENTS

¼ cup graham cracker crumbs

1 tablespoon butter, melted

2 ounces (about ¼ cup) cream cheese, softened

2 tablespoons granulated sugar

½ teaspoon vanilla extract

½ cup heavy cream

½ cup sliced fresh strawberries, hulled

1. Pour crumbs into a small bowl and stir in melted butter. Spoon crumbs into a 8" round dessert dish, press down into a crust, and set aside.

2. In a separate medium bowl, mix together cream cheese, sugar, and vanilla and set aside.

3. Pour heavy cream into the bowl of a stand mixer or medium mixing bowl and whisk until stiff peaks form, about 4 minutes. Gently fold in strawberries.

4. Pour whipped cream mixture into cream cheese mixture and stir well.

5. Spoon mixture over graham cracker crust, cover, and refrigerate at least 20 minutes before enjoying.

PER SERVING

Calories: 946
Fat: 77g
Protein: 9g
Sodium: 328mg

Fiber: 3g
Carbohydrates: 58g
Sugar: 41g

PECAN PIE

SERVES 1 | PREP: 15 MINUTES | COOK: 45 MINUTES

 This small-batch recipe has all the flavors you love in a classic pecan pie. With a buttery shortbread crust and a rich, pecan filling, it is perfect by itself or topped with whipped cream.

INGREDIENTS

For Shortbread Crust

2½ tablespoons softened butter

2 tablespoons granulated sugar

¼ cup all-purpose flour

1 tablespoon cornstarch

⅛ teaspoon kosher salt

For Filling

¼ cup corn syrup

1 large egg

¼ cup granulated sugar

⅛ teaspoon kosher salt

1 tablespoon unsalted butter, melted

½ teaspoon vanilla extract

⅓ cup whole pecans

1. **To make Crust:** Preheat oven to 350°F.

2. In a medium bowl, cream butter and sugar until light and fluffy. Mix in flour, cornstarch, and salt. Press into bottom of a 5" × 5" baking dish lightly greased with butter or oil.

3. Bake 14 minutes until light golden. Set aside.

1. **To make Filling:** Mix corn syrup, egg, sugar, salt, butter, and vanilla together in a medium bowl. Stir in pecans. Pour filling over shortbread crust.

2. Bake on center rack of oven 30 minutes.

3. Remove from oven and let pie cool on a wire rack 2 hours before eating.

PER SERVING

Calories: 1,371
Fat: 72g
Protein: 13g
Sodium: 715mg

Fiber: 4g
Carbohydrates: 180g
Sugar: 145g

SMALL-BATCH OATMEAL RAISIN COOKIES

MAKES 4 COOKIES | PREP: 10 MINUTES | COOK: 10 MINUTES

 These Small-Batch Oatmeal Raisin Cookies are delicious treats you'll keep coming back to. The recipe will yield four standard-sized cookies. If you decide to share with loved ones, the ingredients can be doubled to make eight cookies.

INGREDIENTS

3 tablespoons butter, melted

4 tablespoons light brown sugar

2 tablespoons granulated sugar

1 large egg yolk

¼ teaspoon vanilla extract

⅓ cup all-purpose flour

¼ teaspoon baking soda

¼ teaspoon ground cinnamon

⅛ teaspoon kosher salt

¼ cup old-fashioned oats

¼ cup raisins

1. Preheat oven to 325°F. Line a small baking sheet with parchment paper.

2. In a medium bowl, cream together butter, brown sugar, and granulated sugar.

3. Beat in egg yolk and vanilla extract until creamy. Set aside.

4. In a separate small bowl, mix together flour, baking soda, cinnamon, and salt.

5. Mix flour mixture into butter mixture. Stir in oats and raisins.

6. Use a medium cookie scoop or small spoon to scoop 4 cookies 2" apart onto baking sheet.

7. Bake 8 minutes.

8. Let cool 5 minutes on sheet then transfer to a cooling rack to finish cooling, about 10 minutes. Enjoy.

How to Correctly Measure Flour for Baking
To measure flour, use a spoon to scoop it into a measuring cup, slightly overfilling the cup. Then, use the back of a knife to level the flour across the top of the cup. If you scoop with the measuring cup itself, the flour gets packed too tightly and you end up with more flour than the recipe calls for.

PER SERVING (1 COOKIE)

Calories: 264   Fiber: 1g
Fat: 10g   Carbohydrates: 41g
Protein: 3g   Sugar: 26g
Sodium: 160mg

ROCKY ROAD FUDGE

 MAKES 6 PIECES | PREP: 5 MINUTES | COOK: 0 MINUTES

One bowl and a microwave are all you need for this scaled-down version of my favorite, easy fudge recipe! Tip: A pretty pan of fudge also makes a lovely gift.

INGREDIENTS

½ cup semi-sweet chocolate chips

6 tablespoons sweetened condensed milk

15 miniature marshmallows

¼ cup chopped walnuts

¼ teaspoon vanilla extract

1. Line a 5" × 5" baking dish with aluminum foil, extending foil over edges of dish. Grease foil with butter or cooking spray. Set aside.

2. Combine chocolate chips and sweetened condensed milk in a medium, microwave-safe bowl. Microwave on high 30 seconds.

3. Remove bowl from microwave and stir until chocolate chips are completely melted. Stir in marshmallows, chopped walnuts, and vanilla.

4. Spread mixture into prepared pan. Cover and refrigerate 1½ hours until firm.

5. Lift fudge from pan using foil ends and cut into squares. Enjoy.

What to Do with Leftover Condensed Milk

You will only need 3 ounces of condensed milk for this recipe. To use the rest, consider adding it to your morning coffee or drizzling over sliced fruit. You can also freeze the condensed milk in an airtight container for up to 3 months. It can be thawed overnight in the refrigerator.

PER SERVING (1 PIECE)

Calories: 166
Fat: 9g
Protein: 3g
Sodium: 27mg

Fiber: 1g
Carbohydrates: 21g
Sugar: 19g

APPLE CRISP

SERVES 1 | PREP: 5 MINUTES | COOK: 25 MINUTES

 This is the easiest, best-tasting Apple Crisp recipe you'll ever find! One apple is baked in brown sugar, cinnamon, and butter underneath a buttery topping. It's the perfect size for one perfect dessert!

INGREDIENTS

For Filling

1 small Red Delicious apple, peeled, cored, and diced

½ teaspoon granulated sugar

⅛ teaspoon ground cinnamon

For Topping

2 tablespoons light brown sugar

2 teaspoons all-purpose flour

½ teaspoon ground cinnamon

1 tablespoon cold butter, cut into pieces

1. **To make Filling:** Preheat oven to 350°F.

2. Place diced apple in an ungreased 8-ounce ramekin. Stir in sugar and cinnamon.

1. **To make Topping:** In a small bowl, whisk together brown sugar, flour, cinnamon, and butter. Toss in butter and use your fingers or a fork to work it into the dry ingredients until heavy crumbs form.

2. Spoon crumb mixture over apples and bake 25 minutes until apples are soft. Enjoy.

PER SERVING

Calories: 299
Fat: 12g
Protein: 1g
Sodium: 4mg

Fiber: 4g
Carbohydrates: 51g
Sugar: 41g

TRES LECHES CAKE

SERVES 1 | PREP: 15 MINUTES | COOK: 30 MINUTES

 A Tres Leches Cake gets its name from the three different kinds of milk it uses. It begins with a tender, buttery sponge cake that is then soaked in sweetened condensed milk, evaporated milk, and cream, and finally topped with fluffy whipped cream and a hint of ground cinnamon. It's surprisingly easy to make, and incredibly delicious.

INGREDIENTS

⅓ cup all-purpose flour

¼ teaspoon baking powder

1 large egg, white and yolk separated

5 tablespoons granulated sugar

2 tablespoons 1% milk

¼ cup heavy cream

¼ cup sweetened condensed milk

2 tablespoons evaporated milk

⅛ teaspoon ground cinnamon

2 tablespoons whipped cream

1. Preheat oven to 350°F. Lightly butter a 10-ounce ramekin and set aside.

2. Mix flour and baking powder in a small bowl. Set aside.

3. In a separate medium bowl, use an electric mixer to whip egg white until foamy. With mixer still running, gradually add sugar and beat until frothy, about 4 minutes.

4. Beat in egg yolk, then add flour mixture in three additions, alternating with milk between each addition. Blend well after each flour and milk addition.

5. Pour batter into ramekin and bake 25 minutes, until a toothpick inserted in the center comes out clean.

6. Remove cake from oven and let cool slightly on a baking rack 10 minutes. Pierce cake all over with the tines of a fork or a thick skewer.

7. In a small bowl, whisk together heavy cream, sweetened condensed milk, evaporated milk, and cinnamon. Pour over cake in a medium bowl. Cover and refrigerate cake at least 3 hours or overnight.

8. When ready to enjoy, top with whipped cream.

PER SERVING

Calories: 1,075   Fiber: 1g
Fat: 47g   Carbohydrates: 144g
Protein: 22g   Sugar: 112g
Sodium: 331mg

PEPPERMINT MERINGUES

SERVES 1 | PREP: 15 MINUTES | COOK: 2 HOURS

 This wonderful Peppermint Meringues recipe will yield six melt-in-your-mouth meringue cookies that are crispy on the outside and wonderfully chewy in the center. It's the perfect recipe to use when you have one egg white left over from another recipe.

INGREDIENTS

1 large egg white

¼ teaspoon cream of tartar

⅓ cup granulated sugar

⅛ teaspoon mint extract

1. Preheat oven to 350°F and line a small baking sheet with parchment paper.

2. In a large bowl, beat egg white with a hand mixer until foamy. Add cream of tartar and beat until fluffy.

3. Add sugar very slowly, 1 tablespoon at a time, while still beating. Add mint extract and continue beating until meringue is stiff and shiny, about 5 minutes.

4. Using a large tablespoon, drop mixture in 6 even circles onto prepared baking sheet.

5. Place baking sheet in oven and turn heat off. Leave cookies undisturbed in oven 2 hours.

6. Remove from oven and store in an airtight container up to 2 weeks until ready to enjoy.

PER SERVING

Calories: 279   Fiber: 0g
Fat: 0g   Carbohydrates: 68g
Protein: 4g   Sugar: 67g
Sodium: 56mg

RUM RAISIN RICE PUDDING

SERVES 1 | PREP: 5 MINUTES | COOK: 25 MINUTES

 There's something incredibly comforting about a bowl of rice pudding. For me, it's also nostalgic, as I have fond memories of my mother making it when I was a little girl. This Rum Raisin Rice Pudding is a unique twist on that traditional rice pudding recipe; the raisins are soaked in rum to add more flavor.

INGREDIENTS

¼ cup raisins

2 tablespoons dark rum

¼ cup white rice

1 cup 1% milk

2 tablespoons granulated sugar

⅛ teaspoon kosher salt

⅛ teaspoon ground cinnamon

¼ teaspoon vanilla extract

½ tablespoon room temperature butter

1. In a small bowl, combine raisins and rum. Set aside.

2. Combine rice, milk, sugar, and salt in a 1-quart saucepan over medium heat. Bring to a boil, stirring occasionally, until rice is tender and pudding is thick, about 20 minutes.

3. Remove from heat and stir in cinnamon, vanilla, raisins, and butter. Enjoy warm.

PER SERVING

Calories: 627
Fat: 9g
Protein: 13g
Sodium: 405mg

Fiber: 2g
Carbohydrates: 111g
Sugar: 62g

CHOCOLATE STRAWBERRY SHORTCAKE

SERVES 1 | PREP: 5 MINUTES | COOK: 15 MINUTES

This Chocolate Strawberry Shortcake recipe is the perfect size to satisfy your sweet tooth. The "biscuit" is slightly sweet thanks to a hint of cinnamon, cocoa powder, and a few chocolate chips, and is served with fresh sliced strawberries and a hefty dollop of whipped cream.

INGREDIENTS

6 tablespoons all-purpose flour

2 tablespoons cocoa powder

1 tablespoon granulated sugar

½ teaspoon baking powder

⅛ teaspoon baking soda

⅛ teaspoon ground cinnamon

⅛ teaspoon kosher salt

2 tablespoons cold butter

2 tablespoons semi-sweet chocolate chips

3 tablespoons 1% milk

¼ cup sliced strawberries

½ cup whipped cream

1. Preheat oven to 400°F.

2. Whisk together flour, cocoa powder, sugar, baking powder, baking soda, cinnamon, and salt in a small bowl.

3. Cut butter into flour mixture using either a pastry blender, a fork, or your fingertips until mixture resembles coarse crumbs.

4. Stir in chocolate chips, then add milk and stir until just combined.

5. Spoon dough onto a baking sheet lined with parchment paper and shape into a circle. Bake 14 minutes until top is golden.

6. Remove from oven and let cool 10 minutes.

7. **To assemble Shortcake:** Slice biscuit in half lengthwise, spoon sliced strawberries on bottom half, and top with whipped cream. Top with remaining biscuit half. Enjoy.

Homemade Whipped Cream

To make your own easy whipped cream, simply pour ¼ cup heavy cream and 1 teaspoon of sugar into a small mixing bowl. Whisk just until the cream reaches soft peaks, about 3 minutes.

PER SERVING

Calories: 787
Fat: 53g
Protein: 12g
Sodium: 675mg

Fiber: 7g
Carbohydrates: 76g
Sugar: 30g

HOT CHOCOLATE

SERVES 1 | PREP: 5 MINUTES | COOK: 10 MINUTES

 This homemade Hot Chocolate recipe delivers a single-serving mug of hot chocolate that is so much richer than the store-bought packets. In fact, it's a scaled-down version of the hot chocolate I made when my children were young; I always had some simmering on the stove during the holidays.

INGREDIENTS

½ cup milk

½ cup heavy cream

2 tablespoons granulated sugar

1 tablespoon unsweetened cocoa powder

⅛ teaspoon ground cinnamon

⅛ teaspoon vanilla extract

1. Pour milk and cream into a small saucepan over medium heat and heat to a simmer.

2. Meanwhile, stir together sugar, cocoa powder, and cinnamon in a small bowl.

3. Stir cocoa mixture into saucepan. Simmer 5 minutes, being careful not to let the milk boil.

4. Remove from heat and stir in vanilla. Pour into a large mug and enjoy.

PER SERVING

Calories: 595   Fiber: 2g
Fat: 48g   Carbohydrates: 38g
Protein: 8g   Sugar: 34g
Sodium: 86mg

APPLE FRITTERS

MAKES 4 FRITTERS | PREP: 15 MINUTES | COOK: 10 MINUTES

 Crispy on the outside and soft with sweet bits of apples on the inside, these Apple Fritters are a delight. Fried in canola oil and dusted with powdered sugar, they're perfect with a tall glass of cold milk. This recipe will yield about four Apple Fritters, depending on how large you make them, and are best when eaten warm.

INGREDIENTS

½ cup all-purpose flour

½ teaspoon baking powder

¼ teaspoon ground cinnamon

¼ teaspoon kosher salt

2 tablespoons granulated sugar

⅛ teaspoon ground nutmeg

¼ cup water

⅓ cup chopped, cored, and seeded red apples

Canola oil for frying

1 teaspoon powdered sugar

1. Combine flour, baking powder, cinnamon, salt, sugar, and nutmeg in a medium bowl. Stir in water, gently fold in apples, and set aside.

2. In a deep, 2-quart saucepan over medium heat, add enough canola oil to come halfway up the sides. Heat to 350°F.

3. Using a large metal spoon, carefully drop dough into oil and fry 4 minutes until golden brown and crispy.

4. Use a slotted spoon to remove fritters from pan and drain on a large paper towel–lined plate.

5. Dust with powdered sugar and enjoy while warm.

PER SERVING (1 FRITTER)

Calories: 458   Fiber: 3g
Fat: 12g   Carbohydrates: 82g
Protein: 7g   Sugar: 32g
Sodium: 765mg

STRAWBERRY GALETTE

SERVES 1 | PREP: 25 MINUTES | COOK: 25 MINUTES

 A galette is a French pastry similar to a tart or pie; pastry dough is wrapped around fresh fruit and baked without a special pan or pie dish. Feel free to top your galette with whipped cream, vanilla ice cream, or an extra dusting of powdered sugar.

INGREDIENTS

For Crust

5 tablespoons all-purpose flour

1 teaspoon granulated sugar

⅛ teaspoon kosher salt

2 tablespoons cold butter

2 teaspoons ice water

For Filling

½ cup sliced fresh strawberries, hulled

1½ teaspoons powdered sugar plus ¼ teaspoon, divided

⅛ teaspoon vanilla extract

1 large egg, beaten

PER SERVING

Calories: 479
Fat: 28g
Protein: 11g
Sodium: 367mg

Fiber: 3g
Carbohydrates: 45g
Sugar: 13g

Preheat oven to 400°F.

1. **To make Crust:** In a small bowl, mix together flour, sugar, and salt. Using a fork, cut in butter until mixture resembles wet sand.

2. Add water and stir to form dough.

3. Turn dough out onto a piece of plastic wrap. Flatten into a disk and wrap completely, then refrigerate 20 minutes.

1. **To make Filling:** While dough is chilling, mix strawberries with 1½ teaspoons powdered sugar and vanilla in a small bowl. Set aside.

2. Unwrap chilled dough and place on a piece of parchment paper. Cover with a second piece of parchment paper. Using a rolling pin, roll dough into a circle 6" in diameter.

3. Place parchment paper with dough onto a large baking sheet. Remove top piece of parchment.

4. Spoon strawberries into center of dough, leaving 1" of dough around sides. Fold rim of dough up and around filling.

5. Brush crust with beaten egg and sprinkle the crust and filling with remaining sugar.

6. Bake 25 minutes, until crust is golden. Enjoy.

SMALL-BATCH CHOCOLATE-DIPPED SHORTBREAD

MAKES 3 COOKIES | PREP: 10 MINUTES | COOK: 15 MINUTES

 The buttery flavor and light texture of shortbread makes it the perfect cookie to enjoy with coffee or tea. An added bonus is it requires very few ingredients, and can be baked quickly. This scaled-down recipe will yield three perfect cookies drizzled in melted chocolate.

INGREDIENTS

¼ cup butter, softened

3 tablespoons granulated sugar plus ¼ teaspoon for topping

¼ teaspoon vanilla extract

½ cup all-purpose flour

2 ounces semi-sweet chocolate

1. Preheat oven to 325°F. Line a small baking sheet with parchment paper.

2. In a small mixing bowl, beat butter, sugar, and vanilla together with a hand mixer until creamy. Add flour and beat until well mixed.

3. Knead mixture 4 times until dough forms a ball. Divide into 3 equally sized balls and place on baking sheet about 3" apart.

4. Using the palm of your hand or a large spoon, gently press down on dough balls so they flatten to about ¼" thickness.

5. Sprinkle ¼ teaspoon sugar evenly over each cookie. Bake 14 minutes.

6. Remove cookies from oven and let cool on baking sheet 5 minutes, then transfer to a cooling rack and cool completely, about 10 minutes.

7. While cookies are cooling, microwave chocolate in small microwaveable bowl on high 30 seconds; stir. Microwave 10 seconds more; stir. Continue heating and stirring in 10-second increments until completely melted.

8. Dip a spoon into melted chocolate. Drizzle chocolate over edges and tops of cookies. Allow chocolate to harden before eating, about 20 minutes.

PER SERVING (1 COOKIE)

Calories: 353	Fiber: 2g
Fat: 21g	Carbohydrates: 41g
Protein: 3g	Sugar: 23g
Sodium: 5mg	

OLD-FASHIONED GINGERBREAD

MAKES 4 SQUARES | PREP: 15 MINUTES | COOK: 30 MINUTES

This wonderful gingerbread recipe is perfect for the holidays—or any time of the year! Gingerbread is a lovely treat to enjoy with coffee or tea, and can be served alone, or topped with a dollop of whipped cream or a dusting of powdered sugar. This recipe yields four small squares of gingerbread that will keep well in an airtight container for up to three days.

INGREDIENTS

2 tablespoons granulated sugar

2 tablespoons butter, softened

1 large egg yolk

¼ cup molasses

⅔ cup all-purpose flour

¼ teaspoon baking soda

¼ teaspoon ground cinnamon

¼ teaspoon ground ginger

⅛ teaspoon ground cloves

⅛ teaspoon kosher salt

¼ cup hot water

1. Preheat oven to 350°F. Grease a 5" × 5" baking dish with butter or oil.

2. In a medium bowl, cream together sugar and butter. Beat in egg yolk, then mix in molasses.

3. In a separate small bowl, whisk together flour, baking soda, cinnamon, ginger, cloves, and salt. Pour into sugar mixture and mix well.

4. Stir in hot water, then pour into prepared baking dish.

5. Bake 30 minutes, until a knife inserted in the center comes out clean.

6. Allow to cool in pan, about 15 minutes before slicing into 4 squares.

PER SERVING (1 SQUARE)

Calories: 228
Fat: 7g
Protein: 4g
Sodium: 178mg

Fiber: 1g
Carbohydrates: 38g
Sugar: 21g

CINNAMON BAKED APPLE

SERVES 1 | PREP: 10 MINUTES | COOK: 40 MINUTES

 When you want an easy, warm, sweet dessert to end the day with, turn to this baked apple recipe! The apple is filled with a dreamy mix of oats, cinnamon, nutmeg, and brown sugar, then topped with a dot of butter. It's a recipe that can also be easily doubled or tripled to share with friends. Dress it up with a scoop of ice cream, a drizzle of chocolate sauce, or whipped cream.

INGREDIENTS

1 tablespoon light brown sugar

2 tablespoons old-fashioned oats

⅛ teaspoon ground cinnamon

⅛ teaspoon ground nutmeg

1 large red apple, cored, with bottom ½" intact

½ tablespoon room temperature butter

¼ cup boiling water

1. Preheat oven to 375°F.

2. Mix brown sugar, oats, cinnamon, and nutmeg in a small bowl. Ensure the well of apple is roughly 1" in diameter, then pack with sugar mixture.

3. Place apple in an ungreased 5" × 5" baking dish and top with butter. Pour hot water into bottom of dish.

4. Bake 35 minutes until apple is cooked through and tender.

5. Remove apple from the oven and spoon juices from bottom of dish over apple in a small bowl. Enjoy.

PER SERVING

Calories: 275
Fat: 7g
Protein: 2g
Sodium: 8mg

Fiber: 7g
Carbohydrates: 54g
Sugar: 37g

S'MORES BROWNIE

SERVES 1 | PREP: 10 MINUTES | COOK: 30 MINUTES

 No need to sit by the fire to enjoy this S'mores Brownie. One large, chewy brownie bakes on top of a buttery graham cracker crust and is topped with melted marshmallows. Yum!

INGREDIENTS

For Crust

½ cup crushed graham crackers

1 teaspoon granulated sugar

1 tablespoon butter, melted

For Brownie

3 tablespoons butter, melted

5 tablespoons granulated sugar

¼ teaspoon vanilla extract

1 large egg yolk

5 tablespoons all-purpose flour

3 tablespoons cocoa powder

⅛ teaspoon baking powder

⅛ teaspoon kosher salt

2 tablespoons semi-sweet chocolate chips

15 miniature marshmallows

1. **To make Crust:** Preheat oven to 325°F.

2. Mix together crumbs, sugar, and butter in a small bowl. Pour into an 8- or 10-ounce ramekin lightly greased with butter or oil and press crumbs into bottom.

3. Put ramekin on a baking sheet, place in oven, and bake 10 minutes. Remove from oven and set aside.

1. **To make Brownie:** Raise the oven temperature to 350°F.

2. In a small bowl, mix together butter and sugar. Stir in vanilla and egg yolk. Add flour, cocoa powder, baking powder, and salt and stir to combine. Fold in the chocolate chips.

3. Pour batter over crust in ramekin. Bake 15 minutes.

4. Remove brownie from oven and top with marshmallows. Bake an additional 8 minutes, until marshmallows are melted and golden brown. Let brownie cool on a wire rack 5 minutes and enjoy warm.

PER SERVING

Calories: 1,254   Fiber: 10g
Fat: 65g   Carbohydrates: 168g
Protein: 15g   Sugar: 98g
Sodium: 596mg

MINI PINEAPPLE UPSIDE-DOWN CAKE

SERVES 1 | PREP: 10 MINUTES | COOK: 30 MINUTES

 This Mini Pineapple Upside-Down Cake is the perfect size for one person! It can be baked in an 8- or 10-ounce ramekin and is so easy to make. You'll need to use only one pineapple slice from a can, so be sure to refrigerate the rest to add to smoothies or overnight oats, or enjoy with a dollop of whipped cream.

INGREDIENTS

For Topping

1 tablespoon butter, melted

1 tablespoon light brown sugar

1 pineapple slice

1 Maraschino cherry

For Cake

1 tablespoon butter, very softened

3 tablespoons granulated sugar

1 large egg yolk

⅛ teaspoon vanilla extract

3 tablespoons all-purpose flour

⅛ teaspoon baking powder

⅛ teaspoon kosher salt

1 tablespoon 1% milk

1. **To make Topping:** Preheat oven to 350°F. Grease sides of an 8- or 10-ounce ramekin with butter.

2. In a small bowl, mix together melted butter and brown sugar. Pour into ramekin and spread so entire bottom of ramekin is covered. Top with pineapple slice and place cherry in center of pineapple. Set aside.

1. **To make Cake:** In a separate small bowl, mix together softened butter and sugar. Add egg yolk and vanilla and mix well.

2. Add flour, baking powder, and salt and stir until just combined. Stir in milk.

3. Pour batter into ramekin and use back of a spoon to smooth over bottom layer. Bake 30 minutes until toothpick inserted into the center comes out clean.

4. Place on a cooling rack to cool 15 minutes, then invert over a medium plate. Enjoy.

PER SERVING

Calories: 655   Fiber: 3g
Fat: 28g   Carbohydrates: 98g
Protein: 7g   Sugar: 74g
Sodium: 372mg

LEMON BARS

MAKES 4 BARS | PREP: 10 MINUTES | COOK: 35 MINUTES

 Made with a buttery shortbread crust, this small-batch recipe yields four small, scrumptious bars: a wonderful amount for one! The classic lemon filling is the perfect balance of tart and sweet. For best results, bake in a 5" × 5" baking dish, or use two 8.5-ounce ramekins.

INGREDIENTS

For Crust

2½ tablespoons butter, softened

2 tablespoons granulated sugar

¼ cup all-purpose flour

1 tablespoon cornstarch

⅛ teaspoon kosher salt

For Lemon Filling

1 large egg

½ cup granulated sugar

1½ tablespoons all-purpose flour

1½ tablespoons lemon juice

Preheat oven to 350°F. Grease a 5" × 5" baking dish or two 8.5-ounce ramekins with butter. Set aside.

1. **To make Crust:** Mix together butter and sugar. Add flour, cornstarch, and salt and mix until combined.

2. Press dough firmly into prepared baking dish or ramekins using back of a spoon. Bake 18 minutes until lightly golden. Remove from the oven and set aside.

1. **To make Filling:** In a small bowl, whisk together egg, sugar, flour, and lemon juice 2 minutes. Pour over crust and bake 16 minutes, until edges begin to brown lightly and center is not jiggly.

2. Remove from oven and transfer to a rack to cool completely, about 15 minutes. Once cooled, cut into 4 bars and enjoy.

PER SERVING (1 BAR)

Calories: 251
Fat: 9g
Protein: 3g
Sodium: 92mg

Fiber: 0g
Carbohydrates: 42g
Sugar: 32g

US/METRIC CONVERSION CHARTS

OVEN TEMP CONVERSIONS

Degrees Fahrenheit	Degrees Celsius
200 degrees F	95 degrees C
250 degrees F	120 degrees C
275 degrees F	135 degrees C
300 degrees F	150 degrees C
325 degrees F	160 degrees C
350 degrees F	180 degrees C
375 degrees F	190 degrees C
400 degrees F	205 degrees C
425 degrees F	220 degrees C
450 degrees F	230 degrees C

VOLUME CONVERSIONS

US Volume Measure	Metric Equivalent
⅛ teaspoon	0.5 milliliter
¼ teaspoon	1 milliliter
½ teaspoon	2 milliliters
1 teaspoon	5 milliliters
½ tablespoon	7 milliliters
1 tablespoon (3 teaspoons)	15 milliliters
2 tablespoons (1 fluid ounce)	30 milliliters
¼ cup (4 tablespoons)	60 milliliters
⅓ cup	90 milliliters
½ cup (4 fluid ounces)	125 milliliters
⅔ cup	160 milliliters
¾ cup (6 fluid ounces)	180 milliliters
1 cup (16 tablespoons)	250 milliliters
1 pint (2 cups)	500 milliliters
1 quart (4 cups)	1 liter (about)

WEIGHT CONVERSIONS

US Weight Measure	Metric Equivalent
½ ounce	15 grams
1 ounce	30 grams
2 ounce	60 grams
3 ounce	85 grams
¼ pound (4 ounces)	115 grams
½ pound (8 ounces)	225 grams
¾ pound (12 ounces)	340 grams
1 pound (16 ounces)	454 grams

BAKING PAN SIZES

American	Metric
8 x 1½ inch round baking pan	20 x 4 cm cake tin
9 x 1½ inch round baking pan	23 x 3.5 cm cake tin
11 x 7 x 1½ inch baking pan	28 x 18 x 4 cm baking tin
13 x 9 x 2 inch baking pan	30 x 20 x 5 cm baking tin
2 quart rectangular baking dish	30 x 20 x 3 cm baking tin
15 x 10 x 2 inch baking pan	30 x 25 x 2 cm baking tin (Swiss roll tin)
9 inch pie plate	22 x 4 or 23 x 4 cm pie plate
7 or 8 inch springform pan	18 or 20 cm springform or loose bottom cake tin
9 x 5 x 3 inch loaf pan	23 x 13 x 7 cm or 2 lb narrow loaf or pâté tin
1½ quart casserole	1.5 liter casserole
2 quart casserole	2 liter casserole

HOW TO REDUCE A RECIPE

Original Amount	Half the Amount	One-Third the Amount
1 cup	½ cup	⅓ cup
¾ cup	6 tablespoons	¼ cup
⅔ cup	⅓ cup	3 tablespoons + 1½ teaspoons
½ cup	¼ cup	2 tablespoons + 2 teaspoons
⅓ cup	2 tablespoons + 2 teaspoons	1 tablespoon + 1¼ teaspoons
¼ cup	2 tablespoons	1 tablespoon + 1 teaspoon
1 tablespoon	1½ teaspoons	1 teaspoon
1 teaspoon	½ teaspoon	¼ teaspoon
½ teaspoon	¼ teaspoon	⅛ teaspoon
¼ teaspoon	⅛ teaspoon	dash

INDEX

ABOUT THE AUTHOR

Joanie Zisk is the creator of OneDishKitchen.com, the number one go-to site for single-serving recipes. Since 2012, *One Dish Kitchen* has been inspiring individuals to nourish both body and soul by providing recipes that are a joy to prepare. Joanie's website is filled with hundreds of easy, flavorful recipes tailored for cooking for one. These are the recipes she cooks for herself when her husband is away on business. Joanie's quiet time in the kitchen is sacred to her. "Cooking for just me is therapeutic and intensely satisfying," Joanie says. "I pour myself a glass of wine, turn on a little music, and get creative with ingredients."

Joanie believes that the simple act of cooking for ourselves is one of the most nurturing, loving things we can do. It's a real form of self-care. She hopes the single-serving and small-batch recipes in *The Ultimate Cooking for One Cookbook* satisfy your craving for a fabulous home-cooked meal, and inspire you to experiment with foods you love. "In the end, I want you to enjoy cooking for yourself because *you* are worth it," Joanie says.